Yesterday, Today, and Forever

YESTERDAY, TODAY, AND FOREVER

The Sacrificial Ministry of Intercession

Brittany V. Smalls

Copyright © 2021 by Brittany V. Smalls
All rights reserved.

No part of this publication may be reproduced or transmitted in any form or by any means, including photocopying, recording, or other electronic or mechanical methods without the prior written permission of the publisher, except in the case of brief quotations embodied in critical reviews and certain other noncommercial uses permitted by copyright law. For permission requests, contact services@brittanysmalls.com.

All Scriptures are from the King James Version with permission unless otherwise stated.

Scriptures taken from The Amplified® Bible, Copyright © 2015 by The Lockman Foundation Used by permission. All rights reserved. (www.lockman.org)

Paperback ISBN: 978-1-7369479-0-6

Available for ordering at www.brittanysmalls.com

Printed in the USA

TABLE OF CONTENTS

Dedications	ix
Acknowledgments	xi
Preface	xiii

Yesterday

CHAPTER ONE
Different from the Start — 5

CHAPTER TWO
Faith as a Stepping Stone — 25

CHAPTER THREE
Sacrifice — 43

Today

CHAPTER FOUR
Depth in Intercession — 67

CHAPTER FIVE
Common Culprits Against the Saints — 81

CHAPTER SIX
Changing the Course — 103

CHAPTER SEVEN
Moving in the Presence — 115

Forever

CHAPTER EIGHT
Dependency — 139

CHAPTER NINE
Confidence for the Journey — 147

CHAPTER TEN
Forever Changed — 151

Remember — 157

About the Author — 159

DEDICATIONS

To my husband: He that finds a wife...has just found a lifetime of reasons to pray. You are my honest keeper, even when you don't want to be.

To my children: Thank you for keeping me going. I love you, and I'll never stop. "For he shall give his angels charge over thee, to keep thee in all thy ways."

To my parents, siblings, and in-laws: Thank you for the load you carried as we were in our Job experience.

To my fellow bondservants, the intercessors: As we stealthily embark on the battlefield, remain steadfast in prayer. Don't relent. Don't retreat. "He shall cover thee with his feathers, and under his wings shalt thou trust: his truth shall be thy shield and buckler."

ACKNOWLEDGMENTS

First, I acknowledge my God, my Savior, and my Comforter. This book was his plan. I pray to have done my best at executing his will.

I thank my parents for raising me to even have an idea of who Jesus Christ is. That isn't to be taken for granted, since so many around the nation and around the world do not get to even mention his name without consequence.

To my husband, my P.P., my best friend, my more-than-enough—you have been so patient with this process, and more than that, you have been so encouraging and loving. Looking back on the things we've endured, I am blessed to have had you by my side every step of the way.

To Aunt Mary, you took the time to have a conversation with me decades ago, and that little bit of time has brought me to a lifetime of thankfulness. I appreciate you holding up the light and calling out my ignorance. If it hadn't been for you then, I would probably still be trying to figure this saved life out. Thank you for being an example of boldness and no-nonsense with the word of God.

To Becky Kennedy, you may have some idea, but you will never know how truly blessed I am to have been in your presence, to have had the privilege to pray under your roof, to glean from your life, and to carry your mantle over my life. When I needed a spiritual mother to teach me, to train me, and to navigate me into acknowledging my call, you came into my life, on time. I am this person because you were the person I needed you to be. Thank you for your prophetic voice, your keen spiritual vision, and your tirelessness in prayer.

To every person who encouraged me through this writing process, may God bless you!

Thank you!

PREFACE

During my journey to knowing and understanding my call from God, I discovered there is no script to fit exactly what occurs along the way. My expectations for life were greatly altered while discovering my purpose and answering the call to intercession. I realized there is no secret formula or perfect prayer that strategically pierces through the spirit realm. This statement doesn't detract from what many great authors have written regarding the subject of how to pray, it's simply a personal belief based on my personal experiences.

Learning about the spiritual aspects of being a Christian, I concluded that effective prayers are comprised of the Word of God and your life's living operating in unison. The number of Scriptures thrown into prayer does not make prayer effective if you aren't living out those Scriptures in faith, love, and humility.

Walking the path of righteousness cultured an appreciation for honesty. Though at times difficult to attain or give, honesty generated much of my life's greatest learning experiences. While figuring out who I was, who I wanted to be, and who God created me to be, honesty was the iron that sharpened my perception. When the revelation of who God is, became evident in my life, that truth provided me an avenue to refocus my sight and look at the events of my life differently. When intercessors are honest with God, we see things spiritually the way they are meant to be seen. Intercessors access places in the spirit realm granted only by the Father's permission.

But gaining that access is a process. I compare my early stages of salvation, to the metamorphosis of a caterpillar into a butterfly.

My process began with my childhood baptism and is carried out to this day. Early in life, I was exposed to the concept of spiritual reality through my upbringing in the South, but I gained an understanding of that reality much later in life.

YESTERDAY, TODAY, AND FOREVER

No matter your age, at some point in life, comprehending the spirit realm as reality is a must. With that admission, came new interactions that introduced me to a life of sacrifice. I've faced trying circumstances and setbacks both natural and spiritual, that created varying outcomes that aided in me being the person I am today.

While I would love to say this is a book of prayers, it is not. This book is not designed to teach you how to pray but to encourage you through the reasons of life in which the question is, why pray? My experiences serve as knowledge, inspiration, motivation, and wisdom for other intercessors and those who are feeling the yearning in the pit of their bellies that you too are tasked with being an intercessor. I want you to keep praying, living, and interceding through the issues of your own life.

My intention is to share my purpose with every person who reads this book. I do this with great hope that your story may also be one of fulfillment in your call, no matter the detours and roadblocks along the way.

Yesterday, Today, and Forever is given to you to address common and uncommon circumstances that may occur in life. As you read, you may realize that being a follower of Christ requires more than a confession. The circumstances mentioned often affect other saints, just as they affected my natural and spiritual growth. I delved deep into my life from birth to my current status, and though I couldn't see it back then, I can attest to it now, that the hand of God was guiding me, beckoning me, and comforting me through every phase of life. Jehovah promised to never leave me nor forsake me. He was with me in my yesterday, he is with me in my now and he will be with me in times to come.

By encouraging intercessors to keep praying through, the objective is to help fellow followers of Christ bridge the gap between life and prayer, so prayer can continue to be a part of our lives and not apart from our lives. Too few young women and men are in the know about their God-created purpose. Having not learned my God-created purpose until adulthood, I know how it feels to think you're in control of your life, only to realize that you have been a wanderer, merely traveling through life on systemic expectations. I decided to offer you a candid look into my life, in hope of helping you find direction and purpose.

Being an intercessor is not an easy walk, nor is it a walk where you can become accustomed to the path. If one is to really undertake the burden an intercessor carries, expect a life of peculiarity and change. Though connected, not all intercessors function alike. I may not sound like you or operate in compliance with the same consecration as you, but the spiritual battle remains the same. Victory is gained by fighting and sacrificing!

If you have already answered the call of intercession, my prayer is for this book to continue pushing you to accomplish your work, knowing that you are not alone. If you are uncertain of your call, my prayer is for you to be introduced to the authenticity of prayer and its impeccable power. I believe praying is the first step to knowing what is required of you.

Following each chapter, I've included prayers Holy Spirit impressed upon me to pray during the writing process, and during the trials of life. They aren't intended to be used or repeated as a standard or specific prayer that will fit every circumstance or situation. The Holy Spirit should lead you to pray for your specific requests and the circumstances or situations surrounding your life. I believe firmly that in all your getting, get an understanding.

Be encouraged, be blessed, and be prayerful,

Brittany V. Smalls

YESTERDAY

We delight in the beauty of the butterfly, but rarely admit the changes it has gone through to achieve that beauty.

–Maya Angelou

CHAPTER ONE

Different from the Start

Remember now thy Creator in the days of thy youth.

Children are taught about the life cycle of a butterfly from its infancy to its adult form. A popular children's story that I've read many times to my children, *The Very Hungry Caterpillar*, offers a colorful depiction of this process. The story tells of an egg that hatches into a caterpillar. The caterpillar has an insatiable appetite, eating its way through various foods each day until finally, it rests and takes on its next phase within a chrysalis. After waiting and waiting, the caterpillar emerges out of the chrysalis into a beautifully arrayed butterfly.

But what that story doesn't tell, and what most children don't get to hear, are the details behind the process of that seemingly simple and majestic transformation. Some questions go unanswered about the life cycle. *How are the colors of the butterfly determined? How long exactly does it take for the butterfly to become a butterfly?*

Like our spiritual walk, we can be told a story that tells of a simple process with a beautiful depiction of a rather complex and complicated reality. Emotions rise up as we realize there are unanswered questions that stem from the story we were told. How life *could* be, *should* be, or *would* be with Christ was often told to me but as I grew into an understanding of who Jesus is, I realized that I was missing vital details. Possibly, you have found yourself searching for answers that you thought were easy to obtain, but as you lived and learned, you realized those answers weren't so easily accessible as others made them seem. I understand, and because of this, I have a greater ability to empathize and sympathize than when I first started my prayer life.

How It All Began

In 1981, my 18-year-old father joined the United States Army. Fresh out of high school, he made the decision to leave family and friends, for an opportunity of having a military career. Being in the military quickly took my father from his country living in South Carolina and introduced him to weeks of basic training in Fort Leonard Wood, Missouri. Basic training happens in phases. His next phase of training brought him back home to Fort Jackson, South Carolina, for Advance Individual Training or AIT. AIT came to an end, but *life* was just beginning. My father's high school girlfriend was pregnant. The news of overseas travel collided with the news of becoming a father. For 18-months, my father would be stationed in Germany.

In April of 1982, while my father was still in Germany, my mom gave birth to twin girls. After his time overseas, he came home, and in March of 1984, he married my mom. That same year, my parents and sisters traveled to Junction City, Kansas, as my father was to be stationed at Fort Riley.

On April 14, 1985, a cold and frigid Kansas morning, my mother gave birth to her third daughter. After having lived in Kansas for over a year, three months after my birth, my parents traveled back to South Carolina and there we remained.

Growing up as the baby girl, having two older sisters who were twins, left me often playing alone. I was a child with quite an imagination. Playing pretend helped me appreciate storytelling. I was known to be a talker, though I was also one who would internalize. Around family, I was me. Around others, I fell silent. Being raised in the late '80s and early '90s, in the South, you were taught to mind your mouth and your behavior in front of company. Having that discipline heightened my observation skills.

Listening and paying attention to what happened around me, particularly facial expressions, and mannerisms would prove beneficial as I aged. As a child, I just considered myself somewhat nosey. I was unconsciously able to remember events based on the clothes a person had on, the way something smelled, or the song playing or being sung. I was genuinely intrigued by the way people expressed themselves.

In grade school, I was always quiet. Being quiet earned me trust that I never asked for.

Teachers would allow me to do special privileges like get in line first, or have a treat, all things that as a child, made you feel super special. And I felt special. Not just at school, but just within myself. From the start, I felt that I was different, in a unique kind of way.

Little Life, Big Decision

Early on, our church had Sunday services on the first and third Sundays, only because our pastor was pastoring two congregations in different places. Eventually, we started having services every Sunday, but in our home, we weren't regular churchgoers. I was about the age of nine when we started attending regularly. Though we weren't every Sunday attendees, we were still active in the children's choir and in different events.

It was the summer of 1992 and the church held its yearly Summer Revival. We had a night service, and at the end of the preaching, the altar call was made and the offer to join the church or to get baptized was extended. I stepped out into the aisle and walked towards the front of the church. The deacons were standing in a semi-circle, and I told my deacon (in the Baptist church, we had assigned deacons) and he informed the pastor that I wanted to be baptized. A few weeks later, at seven years old, I was baptized.

On the Sunday of my baptism, I remember standing before the congregation as the pastor asked me a series of questions. All was well until the choir began to sing, "Take Me to the Water," a popular Negro Spiritual that was regularly sung at baptisms.

I noticed a shift in the atmosphere, and I wondered if it was just me, or could everyone sense it. I consider this day as being my first spiritual experience because as the choir sang, my pastor leaned down and asked if I believed in Jesus Christ and that he died for me. I answered yes, but there was a tremble in my voice. Tears welled up in my eyes and I began to cry. The pastor hugged me and said, "That's all right." The way he said it made me cry more.

Through the blurriness of my vision, I could see smiling faces along with nodding heads. The children on the front row were smiling, but their smiles were smirks of child-like discomfort mixed with childish humor. I ignored them. I was in tune with what was happening more than I could display.

At that moment, there was an unmistakable, outside-of-my-control feeling, which let me know, "I'm doing the right thing, at the right time, for a reason beyond tradition." I remember thinking about my grandmother, who passed a few years prior. I didn't know much about her spiritual life, nor did I ever think to ask until I started writing this book. When I inquired of my mom and aunt about her, I learned that my grandmother was also known for having a unique spiritual awareness. They noted different times in which she would be able to see angels and their foes. Hearing about my grandmother was like that moment during my baptism, I cried like a baby.

I felt that my decision to get baptized was honored by God and recognized by him as an act of duty. What I didn't know, was that the decision to honor God through baptism would jump-start my spiritual journey.

SUFFICIENT BUT NOT SATISFIED

Though I got baptized, there was little difference for me as a child. I went to school as normal, went on within my family as normal, and continued being me. In my mature yet immature seven-year-old mind, I believed I had forever to do whatever. I saw and heard a lot of things from a lot of people, not all good and certainly not all bad. As the adults in my life became more aware of and involved in Christ-like practices, I observed those as well. My point here is children see and hear what is happening in and out of the home.

As adults, we can't operate as if children do not know what's going on. We can't expect them to be active members of the body of Christ if we haven't taught them or demonstrated to them the basic principles for godly living. When we know better, we are responsible for doing better.

Though my baptism was sincere and special for me, I wasn't aware of how to live for God or what living for God meant. The life that I lived was sufficient because it was routine. But as the saying goes, 'time is a good teacher'; I had plenty of learning and growing to do. As a preteen and into my teenage years, I started to understand that sufficient doesn't mean satisfied.

As years went by, I continued attending church and participating with the hope of learning what living for God meant. I agreed to lead the youth by undertaking the responsibility of our youth choir and assisting with church announcements. While working with the youth, I discovered I enjoyed public speaking. Being a teenager nearing adulthood, I took church more seriously, so I participated in many things. My desire to learn about Jesus intensified and I learned the importance of prayer. Let me stop here.

There is a difference between knowing the importance of prayer and knowing how to pray. I learned that prayer was important, but I wasn't in a mindset of faith to understand why or operate in how to pray. I knew prayer had significant worth because I heard testimonies of others admitting they prayed for something and what they prayed for happened. I believed what I heard. This is evidence of the importance of prayer. However, believing the testimony and being genuinely happy for the person, didn't make me better at praying or understanding how that individual received their blessing. Trusting what I heard but not knowing how to implement the technique, in this case, how to pray, left me ignorant and non-effective.

Effective prayer produces the desired outcome. James 5:16-18 reads: "Confess your faults one to another, and pray one for another, that ye may be healed. The effectual fervent prayer of a righteous man availeth much. Elias was a man subject to like passions as we are, and he prayed earnestly that it might not rain: and it rained not on the earth by the space of three years and six months. And he prayed again, and the heaven gave rain, and the earth brought forth her fruit."

This Scripture is a great example of a prayer that produces. I was not at this place in my life. I prayed as I knew how and yet, it wasn't until much later in my walk that I received results in prayer.

I wanted more. Rehearsing the Lord's Prayer in Sunday school and listening to deacons repeat the same prayer Sunday after Sunday wasn't edifying. It was familiar. God was calling me to the unfamiliar.

On my quest for spiritual growth, I began to fellowship with other churches, though I wasn't sure what I was looking for. To say the least, I became frustrated. I was entering a pivotal point in my life becoming an adult, which required maturity, and I felt very immature in my search. I had no direction, nor did I know how to express myself regarding what I really wanted.

Little did I know, God was using (and continues to use) the most uncomfortable circumstances of my life to drive me toward his will. I let my frustration serve as an opportunity to discover the God of purpose. I knew my life was headed for something abnormal. I say abnormal because my normal didn't involve real salvation. My normal was to be a good person, to treat others right by a standard of moral kindness, and to not drink, smoke, or go to nightclubs. While these practices make for a good lifestyle, those personal habits don't equate to salvation.

Saved or not, I identified as Christian. My belief was in God. I considered myself to be a Christian because I certainly wasn't going to admit to being anything else. However, believing isn't only about thought. It's about action. I wasn't actively living out salvation.

LIBERATING KNOWLEDGE

My senior year of high school approached quickly and sparked a much-needed change in my perspective about salvation. The summer before school began, I worked as a receptionist at a cosmetology school. One afternoon, a student asked if I was saved. I remember jerking my head back and saying, "No! Why would you think that?"

With surprise in her voice, she replied, "I thought you were saved because you wore skirts to work." I laughed at her assumption and told her I dressed this way for professional purposes only.

Later, my aunt, who was an instructor at the school, stopped to talk with me. The conversation reached her, and she wanted to know if it were true. She asked if I was saved and I responded, "No. I'm not one of *those* people."

"What do you mean by *those* people?"

"The people who wear long skirts and are mean and nasty to everyone."

I spoke with such contempt because of my witness of *those* people. I grew up watching the women, especially, be this way.

They were never wearing a smile; they were never pleasant to talk to or even be around. The girls who were raised to not wear pants would sneak them in their bookbags and change at school. To me, this was crazy. I would watch their behavior and wonder, "How did they even get the pants?"

My aunt looked at me and said, "Is that what you think it means to be saved?"

I shared with her how I was nicer and more kindhearted than most of *those* people. If being saved made me like *them*, then I didn't want to be saved. Recalling that summer, I am so grateful for God's mercy. He could have left me in my foolish thinking.

I thank God for the encounter with my aunt. My ignorance coupled with my inexperience in life seeped through my words.

She explained to me how being saved wasn't about my attire or my outlook on another person's life. After giving me the biblical context of being saved based on Romans 10:9, I said, "Hmm…I guess I am then!"

Through my confession and baptism many years earlier, I was already a believer in Jesus Christ. However, there were many things I didn't know nor thought about.

While on my search to discovering how I could attain a prayer life that yields results, this was my most life-changing find. Before that summer, I had a warped and narrow view of Christ being an active part of my life. Realizing salvation was not predicated upon my clothing or my jewelry selection or anything to do with my outer appearance, I now had the freedom to move forward in the pursuit of change.

With this liberation, I had to get acclimated with how to live this life. I was still unsure about prayer on an effective level, due to not yet completely coming into the knowledge of who I was or who Jesus Christ was in my life. I knew he was born in a manger. I read he was the crucified Savior.

However, I was yet to have a personal encounter with Jesus.

Even after understanding what it meant to be saved, I was still catering to a lifestyle of good works. A good works mentality says, "If I do the most good, then I will yield the best in results." The truth is, that's a lie. Changing this type of mindset was tough for me.

Proverbs 16:8 AMP reads, "Better is a little with righteousness than great income [gained] with injustice."

Just as I was then, are so many young adults today. They are challenged by the abrupt reality of adulthood. Even more, adulthood can be traumatizing to the individual if they have been raised to believe all you must do to be successful in life is obtain a good education and get a good job. Honestly, not to input politics and statistics here, but it goes without saying, the student loan debt crisis is tragic. Many went to great schools in hopes of getting a top-notch job and are now working in a field or at a job that has nothing to do with their degree. Those persons are witnessing a completely different reality. As did I.

Don't misunderstand me. Earning a college degree and obtaining a well-paying job is wonderful, but your alumni status and where you work is not a "Get-Out-of-Trouble Free" card for life. Just because you have attained a certain level of education or have received high praise and accolades from your peers or co-workers, you're not excluded from heartache and hardship. I had to get this fact in my head. Death is a non-discriminator. Poverty didn't care about my age or my past successes.

Jesus says, "The thief cometh not, but for to steal, and to kill, and to destroy: I am come that they might have life and that they might have it more abundantly."

You can have a successful mountaintop experience *without* Jesus. You can achieve prominence and status *without* any thought of salvation. Unlike temporary gain, Jesus gives life which is everlasting and abundant. I pray regularly that God gives me my daily bread: what I need, in the amount needed. Doing this helps me be more on the alert of lustful desires of gain without Christ.

I realized no matter how good I thought I was, I was still a sinner by default, filled with obliviousness and a lack of knowledge. I had to repent.

Again, Jesus sets the record straight saying, "Why callest thou me good? There is none good but one, that is, God."

It is easy to walk into a God-thing and have no idea what you're doing or that it is even a God-thing. I was walking into becoming a completely different person than what I grew up like. I desired to know Jesus personally and more intimately. I had to change my mindset. It took years for me to get over having a by-my-works mentality. No job, no amount of money and no amount of charitable works could save me or lead me to Jesus.

As you are finding your listening ear and setting it to the voice of God, don't mistake the experiences you've gone through as frivolous. Indeed, the lessons I learned as a youth created a bridge for the road I was to travel on.

"It is easy to walk into a God-thing and have no idea what you're doing or that it is even a God-thing."

Prayer

Father God, I come to you in the name of my Lord and Savior, Jesus Christ. I acknowledge I have not known you, nor have I acknowledged you in the past. Today, I acknowledge I belong to you. I acknowledge I need you to teach me what pleases you. Teach me, I pray, how to read your word and how to study your word. I pray I can grow into the person you predestined me to be. I pray my past ignorance will not cause me to be hardened or stubborn towards the changes you have in store for my life. I thank you for saving my life, for forgiving my sins, and for loving me. Thank you, God. It's in Jesus's name I pray this. Amen.

CHAPTER TWO

Faith as a Stepping-Stone

But without faith it is impossible to please him...

As indicated in Chapter One, while a caterpillar is preparing to become a butterfly, it requires plenty of food before entering the chrysalis stage. Likewise, with our natural growth, our appetite also increases to sustain our growing, changing body while in preparation for what we are to become. The early stages of seeking out how to pray set me up for the engaging experience of talking with God.

PREPARING FOR NEXT

Entering my freshman year of college, I purposely entertained the idea of letting Jesus change my thinking. I wanted to gather as much information about this new life as I could. I welcomed knowledge, and when I didn't know what I needed to learn, the Lord was gracious enough to introduce me to people who knew a bit more than myself.

Having grown up Baptist, I didn't understand some of the practices of other denominations. While I was learned in aspects concerning the church and the basic principles of obeying and believing, I was a novice in most other areas.

Some things weren't explicitly preached in our services, such as the Holy Spirit as a part of salvation, the manifestation of spiritual power, and speaking in tongues. There were no demonstrations of the gifts of the Spirit as mentioned in First Corinthians 12.

During this time, God orchestrated a set of Christian friends to be a part of my life. It was through them, I was introduced to the idea of being filled with the Holy Spirit and the diversities of spiritual gifts. These were all new things I didn't know to explore. However, God knew what weaponry I would need for the journey ahead. He began to equip me little by little—and at times, with an outpouring.

In my sophomore year of college, my mom received a revival invitation from my aunt, the same aunt who enlightened me regarding salvation. My mom told me about it, and I agreed to go to the service with her. At this time, my aunt was on her way to becoming an ordained minister in the African Methodist Episcopal Church. At the service, the guest evangelist called me and other women out of the congregation to be seated in different locations within the church. I had no idea what was going to happen. Nothing like this had happened to me before in any church setting.

When she finished preaching, she did an altar call for those who needed prayer, and she called the women she repositioned during the service to come up so she could pray for us. This night marked my second most memorable spiritual encounter. I recall the evangelist calling us up, and one by one, she prayed for us.

Nothing about what came next was expected. When it was my turn, I stepped forward and lifted my hands. I cannot tell you what she spoke. I know she pronounced great things over me, and she barely laid a finger on me, if she touched me at all. Suddenly, I was on the floor. I was under the power of the Holy Spirit.

The best way to describe what I was experiencing at that time is: amazing, powerful, and unexplainable. I believe God was letting me know that he was drawing me in. After I fell, I was helped to my feet by the altar workers. I was slightly disoriented but unharmed, and it took a few minutes for me to come to terms with what had taken place. I left service with my mom and she asked me what I thought was happening. I couldn't really explain, but I had a new appreciation for the work of the Spirit. I had an assurance I was on the right track in my spiritual life.

As time progressed, at the end of my junior year of college, going into my senior year, I mostly visited other churches. Though I had not officially left my home church on paper, I was certainly gone in other aspects. I would visit my home church for programs and other functions, but when I returned, my spiritual growth stuck out like a sore thumb. The places I visited showed me young people could be in love with Jesus and operate with the anointing of the Holy Spirit.

I never experienced such an active display of zeal amongst youth and young adults. Growing up in my church, we barely wanted to sing in the choir. We didn't shout, we didn't praise, and we didn't enjoy church as children. This was early to mid-'90s, so church today, is and was not the way it was back then. Youth of my era went to church because we were made to go.

Though I had grown out of my childhood church life, I knew I had so much more to learn. I discovered you don't know what you don't know until you learn what you thought you knew.

I saw other young adult believers behave comfortably in Christ, but I still felt extremely uncomfortable. I didn't know the dos and don'ts of spiritual things. I was yet learning how to pray, and that was becoming a trudge uphill. After speaking with my girlfriends about their faith, they invited me to Bible study. I previously visited churches I was familiar with, and this invitation was to a church I was not familiar with. I decided to step out in faith and join them for Bible study.

When I entered the church, I saw a group of men sitting at a table with their Bibles, and they were speaking to the audience members one by one. This service was not like any Bible study I had known.

I began to wonder what was happening, and just then, the pastor announced this was a Prophetic Directives night. These men were speaking prophetically into the lives of those who were seeking answers from God. Each person had something to share about the individual standing before them. I was very apprehensive about asking a stranger to tell me what God had to say about my life. I decided to lay my apprehension aside and ask a question regarding my future endeavors as a journalist. Surprisingly, only one person had something to say, whereas, before, everyone at the table had plenty to say to the other individuals.

This was an unnerving experience. The information given was accurate. After receiving this word of prophecy, something inside of me shifted. I left the church and drove home confident God was requiring of me to live a different life. I knew I needed to be in an atmosphere like this, to gain access to what I saw demonstrated by the panel of men. That night, I made up my mind to leave my home church. I decided to give faith a try, using it to make sense of the senseless.

STEP BY STEP

I was being called by God and I wanted to answer the call, but I wasn't sure what the call was. I knew I couldn't learn it or figure it out in the place where I was comfortable. I realized I was trying to put new wine into an old wineskin. I had to be open to experiencing God in a different setting amongst a different group of people with various backgrounds. As many of you already know, the spirit of familiarity is often the reason for stunted growth. I now know as a person of prayer, God will require you to go to depths and zones spiritually you may have never thought possible to venture. If I were to be obedient to God, I had to lose my idea of normal and embrace the concept of walking by faith.

By stepping away from comfort and placing my confidence in Jesus Christ, things immediately became noticeably different. The church I joined was non-denominational. Aside from the obvious, meaning it did not belong to a denomination, I had no idea what else this meant for the church. I was used to fellowshipping with churches that were more traditional in nature, and this church was anything but traditional.

Nevertheless, I had great expectations of learning about the different aspects of God and his character in ways I had not thought of before.

At this new church, it wasn't unusual to have prophecy administered before, during, or after the sermon. One Sunday service, the minister began to prophesy, telling others what "thus said the Lord." I wondered how he was able to hear the voice of God. I was back in the same state I found myself in during my ignorance regarding prayer. I believed what they had to say, but I didn't know how they were able to hear beyond the natural.

Therefore, I set my spiritual growth on being able to hear the voice of God. I decided this was a great place to start because trying to figure out the best method of praying would require me to know if God was talking to me as well.

Making this decision would cause a lot of frustrations. When I don't know something, I ask questions, and during this time in my life, I had several questions such as, how was I to know I was hearing God's voice? What did I need to do to be completely certain it wasn't my own thinking? I wanted to formulate a relationship with God that wasn't one-sided. This required communication, and I felt my communication with God was broken. Not because I wasn't trying to communicate, but because I didn't know if my communication was effective.

When I would ask other believers about hearing God's voice, I was simply told to pray about it. I was still on the road to learning how to pray effectively, and now I had to add a pit stop along the way. Seemingly, every question I had about learning to hear the voice of God led me to the same response: *"Pray about it."*

My lack of knowledge and my millennial mindset created the perfect concoction for aggravation and annoyance in this new life in Christ. I was not pleased with the lack of direction I was given. I felt like telling me to pray about it, was just a way to avoid my question, while using this response to pass as spiritual instruction. I interpreted this to mean that no one knew the answers to my questions. I felt I deserved more—more time, more attention, more access. I was getting fed up, fast. I was ready to be on to a real church in a real hurry.

But I knew God had me here. I also knew I was set to a different rhythm. I had this pacing going on and it was driving me to find what I needed to know. In my infancy of spiritual matters, I couldn't put this into words. I'll admit, I was very stubborn, and I was full of pride. This combination blinded me from seeing the direction in which God was taking me. I tell you this because I believe in being honest. After all, honesty released me from stupidity and foolishness. I pray, through my honesty, you can relate and be released as well or help someone else get their release.

It doesn't matter how long ago you accepted Christ into your life or how often you pray. We must all take regular self-examinations of our souls. Pride comes in and seeks to take root. If you don't recognize it and no one has been able to call you on it, much like me, you'll find yourself annoyed and thinking others don't have it together. I'll go a little deeper with pride later in the book but know this: you can be duped. I thought everyone else wasn't getting it when, in fact, it was me who needed to trim off some fat by shedding off my own self.

Again, I was frustrated with how my want for spiritual growth was seemingly being ignored. However, I took this as a challenge. If I couldn't get a straight answer from anyone in the church, I would just figure it out on my own. As many of you already know, yes, this is a rotten attitude. But that kind of attitude led me down the road where I realized I had to become unlearned to learn.

I was trying to bring my self-absorbed thought process into a God-thing. I was foolish to think my unbridled tongue was going to be able to hold a decent conversation with the heavenly Father. I had to give up my logic and my natural understanding to approach the Sovereign God decently and orderly. I had to put my flesh under subjection. It was a struggle, but I wanted God.

As I became obedient with the rudiments of faith,

bit by bit, God began to usher me closer to him. Learning obedience led me to fast. This was new to me and it was difficult. When you are not used to disobeying your flesh, especially when it comes to food, you find out how real this spiritual life can be. I was being conditioned for spiritual authority, whether I understood it then or not. God already knew what I was striving to figure out. He is all-knowing and all-wise. I was all-wondering. Wondering, how was it going to happen? Wondering, why? Wondering, how long would it take? Wondering, when would I finally be mature in Christ?

Finally, after much waiting and wondering, I received a message of hope. The Lord sent a visiting evangelist to our morning service. After she preached the word, she called the members of the church forward for prayer and began to minister to the group. While we gathered in a circle, she would declare to me, I was to pray! No explanation, but explicitly stating, I was to pray. She came to me three times, each time, passionately asserting, "You, pray!"

I took this exactly as it was said. After all, it's what

I was told to do for quite some time. This time, it had a boisterous ring of truth behind it. I heard it differently and after this encounter with her, I began to foster an appreciation for the assignment of prayer. I viewed it as a God-given task rather than a dismissive suggestion given in times past.

I took to the assignment immediately. I began praying for what I had on my mind and heart. I had no Scripture verses memorized, nor did I have an outline to follow. I opened my mouth and talked to God as if I were talking to anyone else—with respect, of course. In doing this, I learned prayer is what I was driven to do all those times I couldn't get a straight answer from others. I was praying but getting stuck on whether I was doing it correctly or not. When I got stuck, I had nothing to get me mentally unstuck. Being stuck affected my understanding of the intent of prayer. I was so distracted by *how* that the *why* began to diminish.

As I continued to pray, leaning more and more into the *why* of prayer rather than the *how* of prayer, I began to desire to know the Holy Spirit and have him living within me. I was yet to be filled, and I knew this was necessary for the life I wanted to experience.

One random day, while leaving school to go to work, a fellow student and brother in Christ stopped me and in our brief conversation, he told me, "When you get home, tell God I said, 'What's up?'" He was known to have the gift of prophecy, and he operated in such an unorthodox manner. I laughed it off, told him I would, and walked away on my way. I worked my shift, and just after 11 o'clock, I found myself at home in bed. I began to pray, and as I was wrapping up what was now my nightly routine, I remembered my conversation earlier with the young man. I chuckled and said to God what he asked of me. As soon as the last word left my lips, my entire mid-section began to quake, and my torso began to quiver and shake uncontrollably. I could distinctly hear different sounding syllables leaving my stammering lips.

I mustered up enough control of myself to pick up the phone and call the young man. He answered right away, and in between stammers, I managed to ask him, "Is this the Holy Ghost?" He replied, "It is! Praise God!" My obvious lack of exposure was apparent, but at the time, it was a seamless transition. It seemed to take a while before I could move from the bed. I didn't want to interrupt the flow of what the Holy Spirit had to say. I didn't understand the language, but I willingly let him speak through me.

In my bedroom, I was filled with the Holy Spirit. It was unexpected, but I thank God he saw fit to endow me outside of the spotlight. It was in my bedroom, a place of lowliness, where He had my complete attention. I praise God for the behind-the-scenes blessings. I have learned those are the sweetest, most precious revelations embedded in my spirit.

After that night of in-filling onward, I have never stopped appreciating the gift of the Holy Spirit. I quickly began maturing in the things of God. The maturation process was not without hiccups along the way, but I accepted even those experiences and charged them as growth spurts.

I later understood my initial gut feeling of being set to a different pace was God's doing. Unbeknownst to me, I was growing quickly in spiritual matters because the Lord was preparing me to be a wife. And not just a wife, which has a spiritual charge connected to its role, but God saw fit to call me to be the wife of a prophet. The same man who spoke into my life at Bible study was chosen by God to be my husband. For prophetic intercessors or those who are prophets or married to prophets, you know this comes with its own challenges and spiritual requirements. I realize the spiritual development and the friendship I gained in my husband, were foundational slabs leading me to acknowledge the call of intercession.

I came to the ministry as a single college student, eager to enter the newness of salvation and learn and connect with God in ways I had never known. Within two years of joining the church, I became a wife and a mother. My husband and I left that ministry shortly after the birth of our son to support the ministry of my father-in-law. I had grown in tremendous ways, but as life would have it, tests became battles, and I was well on my way down a road of sacrifice, whether I wanted it or not.

"*By stepping away from comfort and walking by faith, things immediately became noticeably different.*"

PRAYER

In all thy ways acknowledge him, and he will direct thy path. (Proverbs 3:6)

Father, it's in the name of Jesus Christ I come to you. I thank you for allowing me to move out of my place of comfort. I thank you for leading me. Your word declares in Psalm 23 that you lead me on the paths of righteousness for your name's sake. God, I don't always know which way to go. I don't always know what you are asking of me, but I will always trust your plan for my life. You are my Creator, and there is no good thing withheld from me. I believe your will is what's best for me. Even when it is difficult for me to obey, I trust your will. Help me today to walk in faith. Help me to submit my will to yours. Help me to grow and learn from you even more. Lord, I desire to be a light in a world of darkness. Help me to operate by faith and not by sight. It is in the name of your Son, Jesus Christ, I pray. Amen.

CHAPTER THREE

Sacrifice

> And the LORD said unto Satan, Behold, all that he hath is in thy power; only upon himself put not forth thine hand.

While in this new life in Christ, I entered new territory. I took on the assignment of motherhood and marriage. As a woman called to the ministry of prayer, this created a natural strain. I was still new to many things, and becoming a parent was the latest topic to figure out. It doesn't matter how spiritual you are, no manuals are offering step-by-step instructions on parenting. All households are different. Economic statuses are different, and beliefs vary from person to person on the roles within the home.

Becoming a parent is a life-changing situation that forces you to figure out who you are and what you stand for. My husband and I were entering uncharted waters. Parenthood is the type of expedition where once you're out there, you must keep rowing, keep steering, and hoping you will be able to get go through the initial concerns of time and inexperience.

In my first few years of parenthood, time became an aggressor. Suggesting availability and then, suddenly, snatching away its presence. Time was determined to do damage to my will. My desire for God didn't burn out because I got married. My desires didn't go away because I became a mom. But time did. To encourage each of you, please know that gender plays no role in being an intercessor. New roles and responsibilities can present very real challenges for your spiritual walk whether male or female. Being a wife and learning that role was just as much a task for me as it was for my husband learning the role of being a husband. We were in a new area of responsibility to each other and to our child.

I am a very practical person, so dismissing common sense is ill-advised. There were very practical transitions that had to take place in my life to manage my new responsibilities. God was able to grow me up in motherhood because I allowed him to be in every area of my life while functioning in common sense. I knew that I could no longer go to every service or be at every event that my husband was preaching or ministering at as a musician.

While grasping hold of my new life, things began to take an unexpected shift. We were having to make some tough decisions. The voice of my mother-in-law rang out in my head: "Next stop, Job!" These words were spoken to me and my husband nearly a year before the birth of our first child. I didn't know what she meant then, but it quickly became evident.

Struggle, lack, sacrifice, and depletion were our portion. Financially, emotionally, and spiritually—you name it, we were experiencing it. The setbacks, the hurdles, and the overall complaint of "What is going on?" threw us into a frenzy. There were occasions in which I didn't know what to say to God. I had no words. I felt stuck. This was different from when I was learning what salvation was all about while learning the value and importance of prayer. This was a new type of stuck. I was living saved and hearing God's voice, but I still couldn't find the answers. During this time, the Holy Spirit spoke to me these life-changing words: *"If you can go through it, someone else can relate to it."*

GO THROUGH IT

The essence of my struggles let me know years later that I can go through terrible times and still be in the will of God. In intercession, it's important to know that what is required of you will not fit the bill of what you are expecting out of life.

With any answered call, there is the requirement of sacrifice. There will be many who would like to boast of being a prayer warrior. To this I say, please do not. I've listened to great persons of prayer and have read many books, and I've come to terms with the fact that intercessors do not go about flaunting the role. Intercessors operate in stealth mode. We do not make our position in prayer known because Satan has spies sent to watch and gather intelligence on the people of God for his corrupted purpose. Intercessors commit to doing what very few are willing to do for themselves—pray without ceasing. I learned being a woman who knows the power of God, is far more humbling than being called a powerful woman of God.

During our Job experience—which was a rather poor time in our lives—I acknowledged my call of intercession and actively walked in it. Most seasons last three to four months. This was a five-year depression. After five years of marriage, the heat was turning up on the trials we faced. Our second child was born, and the financial and emotional stress of life was kicking our butts. Through the constant lack and spiritual depletion, we persisted. We continued to go and serve.

Church services were great, but we were riding the waves. Others around us were being blessed, feeling the power of the anointing, and we were in a low place. We stayed in constant spiritual battle mode. And being in such warfare, we yearned for God to speak to us concerning this season of long-suffering.

Ironically, we were not completely forgotten by

God. It was during this season that I witnessed miracles in the lives of others. These were the types of signs and wonders I heard of and read about but wondered if I'd get the opportunity to observe. I was blessed to have witnessed different accounts of healing and deliverance from demonic spirits, even while we were in our lowly state.

In the thick of our natural depression, God was enriching my spiritual development through these encounters.

It's a known fact that for a seed to grow, it must be placed in dirt and stay in the darkness and coldness of the underground until it receives proper watering and the necessary amount of sunlight before it breaks forth and starts the germination process.

Like a seed, planted and left in the roughest of conditions, I began to grow and develop knowledge of spiritual matters. Despite the muck of our circumstances, God was allowing me to cultivate an authentic testimony. My purpose was being spun out on His great wheel. Uncomfortable? Yes. Difficult? Yes. Worth it? Yes. Did I know or understand this then? No.

There were points in this season when pastors and ministers would speak directly to my husband and me with encouragement and words of knowledge regarding our situation. They would remind us that our latter would be greater.

However, staying strong in His will was hard. As a young wife and mother, I had been suffering from tiredness and sleepless nights. No matter what time it was, no matter what routine I tried to set for myself, no matter what foods I ate, I never had enough energy. I became anxious. The bills were piling up and I didn't work, in part because we couldn't afford the cost of childcare if I did. With only one income supporting the household, every dollar was stretched to ensure food was on the table. This created stress in the marriage because it pained me to see my husband frustrated at not being able to provide for his family in a way he desired.

New clothes were not new and eating out was never an option. I remember calling for supplemental assistance to aid in our food costs. I was told by a representative that because my husband was a teacher, based on his income, I would need to have *another* child to qualify.

In essence, I was too well-off to get assistance, but if I had another baby, I'd be just poor enough. This angered me and served as another reminder of how I couldn't catch a break.

Every month on the first of the month, I became fretful. I would have to call the landlord and ask for an extension on our rent. Not only did I have to make this call to the landlord, but I had to contact the water and utility companies as well. Every time I made these calls, I felt less in control of my life. I felt like a puppet being manipulated by string, and the landlord, the water company, and the utility department were the puppet masters. I was under the impression from the sayings of the elders in the church that when you get saved, your life changes for the better. Looking on the natural side of life, I could not see better. This was not abundant living. I only saw desperation.

In my valley, there were many different signs of witchcraft taking place. As a teaching point for those who might not be aware, you do not have to be in connection, communication, or even doing anything wrong, for those who render satanic practices to be on your radar. Remember that Job was perfect and upright, and feared God, and had nothing to do with evil. Yet, Satan was able, *with permission*, to attack Job. He caused harm to his family, destroyed his way of providing for his family, and even brought hurt to those who worked for Job as servants.

Like Job, we didn't do anything wrong. In fact, despite our circumstances, we were yet hoping and praying for a turnaround. Much like Job, God allowed us to experience what we went through as a testimony of belonging to God. Satan came to prove to God that we would not be faithful servants. He came to spit at us and mock us and discredit our confession. It was up to us, as the children of God, to make Satan a liar!

Do not count your tribulation for naught. There's a time for all things, and in warfare, there is no time for pleasantries.

I was living for Christ and still found myself depressed and ashamed. The body of Christ must be healthy to continue advancing the kingdom of God. Therefore, there should be no judgment in your prayers for others, especially for the saints. Satan tempted Jesus after many days of fasting and praying, and we are not excluded from his slippery schemes.

I encourage you to know that if you are experiencing hardship and turbulence right now while you're on your face for another, please know that I know what you're feeling and how difficult this time can be. Go through it while holding on to God's unchanging hand.

NO WEAPON FORMED SHALL PROSPER

Because the devil is full of filth, he desired to project his filthy, evil ways into our lives.

In our tiny two-bedroom mobile home, there were different times I had to call the maintenance man out due to a foul odor in the house. When I opened the front door to let him in, he could smell it before crossing the threshold. He checked all around but couldn't find the source of the smell. Finally, he went under the house. When he came back, he told me there were two dead cats under the house. I immediately questioned how they got under the house. There was no visible opening or issues with the underpinning. He was just as shocked as I was, and had no answers. A few months later, I had to call him out again because the smell had returned. When he came to check, he found another dead cat under the house. Now, I'm not a fan of cats, but I do acknowledge that the creatures are rather intelligent. You would figure the same way it got in, it would get out. But somehow, this was not the case. Naturally, this was puzzling. Spiritually, it was plain to see what was happening.

Not only did we have the cat situation, but on other occasions, we had snakes, dead birds, and dead rodents. To a person who has not been subjected to demonic activity or witchcraft, this would seem far-fetched or coincidental. The mind would have you rationalize all the reasons why these creatures would appear in the way they did. However, with the spirit of discernment and much prayer, the Holy Spirit has taught me these occurrences were not coincidental.

When I wasn't faced with a dead animal, I was in prayer trying to unravel the will of God for our lives. While praying, it became clear that others had undue influences over our lives and the decisions we were trying to make. This is why it is ever so important to pray *God's* will be done. Within our human nature, our best intentions for someone is not necessarily God's will, but what we would personally like the outcome to be.

A major personal issue for me during this time of motherhood was seeing how all the hard knocks affected the household. Warring in prayer can be laborious and fasting can drain the flesh. Often, I was exhausted. I couldn't wait for God to deliver me from this nightmare called reality. I was worried and perplexed at the hand we were dealt. The natural side of life continued to push me, poke fun at me, and nag me to no end. It was now time to deal with me again—the me God had covered so well with His mighty presence, allowing only him to know my frustrations.

AND THE BUTTERFLY EMERGES

I've learned along the way that it's in the area of your greatest anointing that you will most often be tried. Job's faith was tried, his love of family, his appreciation, and thankfulness toward God were put to the test. And yet, he prevailed!

I contended with the spirit of pride and various stigmas related to poverty and motherhood in my prayer time. Pride comes in many forms. A shapeshifter of sorts. Pride held me back from asking for help, and then, when I fought through and finally asked for help, pride would whisper, "If you're really praying, then why aren't you receiving?"

Pride accompanies the lie that says, "Saints who are really saints don't experience these types of hardships." The image of what a Christian should look like always bothered me. This was another personal issue I had to be willing to release. The thought of, "I'm serving the God of abundant riches, and he's the God who owns the cattle on a thousand hills, why can't I afford ground beef?"

Satan continued to get my emotions out of sorts, and he used this to his advantage.

I was given a test in growth without a study guide. As intercessors, when we are dealing with spiritual deprivation, it is not always an attack.

There are times when we enter a point of inflection in the spirit realm. Inflection is the act or result of curving or bending. Because the term is synonymous with the word bend, I immediately think of my more youthful days, hearing the church mothers say, "You might bend, but you won't break." When we go through our low points, we aren't necessarily at a breaking point. We are bending. We are maneuvering into position. We are stretching and readjusting to fit into the will of God.

In the secret place of the Most High, there comes a point when you are going to be stretched and maneuvered in such a way you no longer respond to situations as you once did. You feel the change, but you don't know what the change is. If you are expecting God to show up familiarly, and he doesn't, you may begin to think you're spiritually off. Likewise, if you're expecting to feel God's presence in a way that is easily recognizable or normal, and it doesn't manifest the way you are expecting it to manifest, you may be tempted to believe you've missed God.

These common feelings are God's way of rooting

out and tearing down the self-made idea of who we are and aligning it with who He is. In these times, God is teaching and demonstrating His sovereignty. I've experienced the highs and lows of trying to figure out what God was up to along with the highs and lows of everyday life. Not knowing what is going on in your life can create frustration and stress. But God will not leave us dumbfounded and without help.

After receiving my personal deliverance, I began to operate differently. However, this only happened after I accepted the fact that I was in constant need of development. The changes that occurred in me spiritually could, at times, be seen outwardly. My tone of voice changed, and I became bolder, more direct, and more intentional with my aim in prayer—all because I reached the point in my walk where God transformed me once again.

Every child of God must go through a spiritual transformation; an intercessor must endure the transformation while transforming situations in the spirit realm on behalf of others. If you haven't traveled the road as an intercessor, but are learning and growing into that call, allow me to tell you this road is by far one of the most selfless journeys one will walk.

As an intercessor, you will have to battle your own natural situations and the spirit of your personal matters while praying for a city, a community, a person, or a congregation. I learned that this is a thankless call, meaning the expectation of acknowledgment should be nonexistent. Your intercession is a charge, not a calling card. It isn't done for fame, but for faithfulness to the Father. I had to rid the concept of personal glory and really kill off my issues of pride. Philippians 2:5-7 says, "Let this mind be in you, which was also in Christ Jesus: Who, being in the form of God, thought it not robbery to be equal with God: But made himself of no reputation, and took upon him the form of a servant."

If you ever find one who claims they are an intercessor and you find them to be pompous, know that they have yet to go through the bending process and come out secured in their appointment. Being humble is a dominant trait in an intercessor; this means humility is always on, but it does not mean that you are any person's doormat.

If you are not an intercessor but are searching for your purpose, keep in the forefront of your mind that as a servant of God, you will go through many transformations as often as is necessary. We are flesh, living in a trying world, and will always require repentance.

Being an intercessor doesn't mean your human nature is evaded by your call. Losing pride, being humble, and walking in the power of light takes consistency in repentance and maturity. Being able to go before the throne of God and being capable of pleading the cause of another or for yourself requires cleanliness. Even if you have had no issues per your knowledge, repent anyway. This eliminates the hassle in the spirit realm as to your worthiness to go against the devil.

I needed encouragement during my forgoing. In the same way, I am encouraging you to continue to be steadfast in the faith. Not all intercessors operate in the same way, and many may never experience the kind of sacrifices I have. Some are skilled specifically for international duty, while others are skilled within their local area. No matter where you are positioned, we all have had and will continue to have sacrifices. The sacrifices that made me came well before the age of 30. Do not think that sacrifice is for only a season. In ways, we will always be sacrificing. It is a part of the life God has chosen for us.

If you are learning the ropes of having a prayer ministry or being an intercessor, know that you will make it through. God will not put more on you than you can bear. If you ever believe your load is too much to carry, be reminded of John 15:16, believing that whatsoever you ask of the Father in his name, he may give it to you.

> *"In this walk, you will go through many transformations as often as necessary."*

PRAYER

Father God, it's in the name of Jesus I come to you. In this season, I need your strength. I love you, Lord. I have seen your hand and I know you are with me. Help me to continue this race. Help me to move beyond what I feel and what the circumstances are like for me and my family. I pray in the name of Jesus Christ, according to Matthew 7:7. I am asking, seeking, and knocking. For when I ask, your word says I will receive it. When I seek, you said I would find it. Lord God, when I knock, you said the door would be opened unto me. I am asking for your hand to guide me through this season and to lead me into a place of your grace. I am seeking your will at this time. Allow me to know what I need to know. Father, I am knocking and expecting you to open the door of overflow in my life so I may extend your kindness to others. I thank you for your promises, and I believe your word. In the name of Jesus Christ, I do pray. Amen.

TODAY

"I learned that courage was not the absence of fear, but the triumph over it. The brave man is not he who does not feel afraid, but he who conquers that fear."

–Nelson Mandela

CHAPTER FOUR

Depth in Intercession

Do not fear [anything], for I am with you; Do not be afraid, for I am your God. I will strengthen you, be assured I will help you; I will certainly take hold of you with My righteous hand [a hand of justice, of power, of victory, of salvation].

I was once terrified of getting into a pool or the ocean. As a young girl, a near-drowning experience at the beach held me captive for years from enjoying the water. Not knowing how to swim and the idea of bottomless water frightened me tremendously.

It wasn't until I had my first child that I made the decision that I would learn to swim. I didn't want to put on my son the fear of the water, therefore, I wanted him to learn to swim as well. I learned that getting into pools inch by inch was better than just diving in. I took the idea of going deeper, slowly. I didn't want to rush through my self-taught training until I could advance confidently. I wanted to be strong enough and capable enough that if the need would ever arise, I could safely remove my son and myself from the water.

I eventually made my way further into the lower end of the pool, but that would've never happened if I remained in fear. Playing it safe was code for, "I'm scared." I couldn't let fear dictate that particular part of my life anymore because it was no longer only affecting my life.

And so it is with intercession. Submitting to the will of God for my life concerning intercession, I knew that there were layers to praying. The essence of intercession is for the act to be done for someone else. I knew that entering the unknown was scary. I didn't know what to expect, but the Holy Spirit guides and leads us inch by inch to where God wills for us to go until we are confident and willing to go there on our own.

GO DEEPER ON PURPOSE

This chapter in particular was a tough one to

write. While preparing this book, I spent months on this chapter with nothing written. I toiled with how much to share, and how to say it. I could feel the Spirit drawing me to a place of transparency and depth, but my flesh was trying so hard to remain on the surface and just write...nice.

One day, I was tired of wondering where this was going, and the Holy Spirit spoke plainly to me: "You're feeling stuck because you're afraid to go to the depth that I'm pulling you to." Needless to say, I cried like a baby, because it was the truth. The realness of God extends beyond a feeling. It goes to the very core of our existence and causes us to have a reason for being.

Praying through when you don't feel like it, is hard. Loving folks that seem to be hard to love, is difficult. I will not pretend that this is a cakewalk. It is a walk that purifies by the opposition we face and grows us step by step.

If you are looking for God to heal deep hurts, to eliminate deep pain, to use you beyond the surface, then you have no choice but to go deeper on purpose. Even with all that you're currently experiencing or have experienced in the past, God is yet requiring depth of perception and in ability.

DISCERN

After enduring the bending process, I now walked in the depth of intercession. I caution you here. If you are struggling with your feelings and are doubtful or unsure of your ability, then stay put! It's easy to drown in something so familiar yet so unknown.

Having come through the thickest part of our troubles, though not completely out, I now understood the difference between God's will, my will, and the will of others for my life. With that understanding came new challenges. While on my first spiritual post of sorts, I fumbled the confidence ball. I thought I was ready, but I quickly realized I was not. I was not in battle gear and I wavered in my ability. I now know I should have never placed my confidence in *my* ability.

In intercession, actions cannot come from a place of self-reliance. If they do, you're not ready for battle. If your faith is lacking, then pray in the Spirit to increase your faith. The point here is for you to handle yourself before entering the zone of prayer where you may experience things you have not seen before.

A vital way of preparing is to walk upright before God. Live a life that doesn't cause your actions nor your words to work against you. In addition to this, also be repentant—whether you think you have a reason to or not. Repentance clears the way for the Lord to approve us by getting rid of the junk polluting our thinking. With our confidence in Christ Jesus, we go into war with assurance.

Entering this next degree of knowledge, I became more aware of the need for living a life of sanctification and consecration. Both are a must for holiness, and you must allow the Holy Spirit to teach what is necessary for your consecrated life. It is not the same for every person. In going deeper into prayer, the Holy Spirit reveals mysteries and allows us to see the enemy for who he is.

There are many types of demons, but the strongman is the master. Through personal experience and lessons taught to me, I know that how a thing appears is not necessarily what it is. On the contrary, how a thing appears can be exactly what it is. You must spend time in prayer and in the word of God to learn the difference.

Remember my dead cat situation? From a carnal mindset, that entire situation would be marked as weird. But here's a good way to learn how to discern using knowledge. First, ask yourself, "Is what I'm seeing or experiencing out of the ordinary?" Next, ask yourself, "Is this causing or bringing me peace or is it making me restless and uncomfortable?" And thirdly, ask yourself, "Is this something that I could attribute as God's Fatherly protection or provision?"

Once you answer these initial questions about your situation, then you can begin unraveling the truth. In my cat fiasco, the truth of the matter was that this was too weird to be coincidental. It happened twice. And not to anyone else's home but ours. In addition to that, the situation was grieving us naturally. The smell was permeating the air to near suffocation. It was aggressive and unpleasant, no deodorizer or air freshener would work. Finally, nothing about this situation in either instance provided any notion that this was God's way of meeting a need in our life. In fact, after the cat situation, there was a mold infestation, which ultimately resulted in us moving.

I've learned and am still learning to discern spirits because the workers of darkness do not only work spiritually but are known for manifesting naturally as well. Demons are not out to make friends; they are on assignment to destroy the lives of those who believe in God and those who do not. If demons can get a soul on their side, by any means, they will.

In Chapter One, I make it clear that early in my Christian experience I lacked spiritual knowledge. I found myself often aggravated with responses to my questions. Not only that but some of the frustration experienced during our "Job" season is attributed to just not knowing what to do.

In that season of depravity, we leaned on family members for most of our needs during that time. Alienation became a key feeling. I would often say, "It seems like everybody is making it, except us." What that translates to is: "Nobody understands what we're going through." Alienation is deception.

The enemy would have you to think that you're all alone, when in fact, you're not. If you buy into his lies, and the feelings that come with his lies, then soon, you'll be speaking his lies and we know the power of words, right? Remember, God had to remind me that if I could go through it, someone else could relate to it.

I count myself blessed to have witnessed the power of God in operation during my time in fellowship with a deliverance ministry. The education on deliverance and the different spirits that can put a soul in bondage has proven an invaluable lesson to this day.

Thankfully, I learned to trust and to depend on others to help me while I continued to grow in this way. If we succumb to division in our individual walk, we risk unity in the entire body.

Revelation 12:17 sums up the plan of Satan. He seeks to wreak havoc on the remnant of God. As intercessors, we are doubly tasked with the charge of applying Scripture and prayer for ourselves and others to fight for the kingdom of God.

The weapons of our warfare are not carnal.

Therefore, we must operate with spiritual understanding and natural strategy. We have to ask for the gift of discerning of spirits so we can move forward in life and not be bound wrestling with "what-ifs."

THE PLACE OF ATTACK

As a child of God, if your head isn't covered with the helmet of salvation, you are likely to fall subject to the mind games of the workers of darkness. The point of taking on the whole armor of God is so that we may be able to withstand in the evil day (Eph. 6:13).

As I said at the beginning of this chapter when I was facing my first spiritual battle, I was not properly dressed, and I lacked the functioning to move with confidence in the Spirit. The armor of God is not merely metaphorical; it is more importantly spiritually applicable.

Because we face days that are filled with evil regularly, take the whole—intact, nothing broken, no parts missing—spiritual armor of God. Your armor is a mighty protective suit. It covers the vital areas more commonly attacked in battle.

Throughout many spiritual battles, I've learned that the mind is one of the main places of attack. We, as Christians, are often terribly busy. Because we are so busy doing and going, our minds tend to go into overdrive. Even worse, we go into overdrive so often that we end up burning out and eventually checking out. This happens because time isn't spent stilling ourselves long enough to renew our natural and spiritual strength.

We've believed the lie that says, "If we aren't busy for God, then we're busy for the devil." Not so! The word of God declares that he "giveth his beloved sleep" (Ps. 127:2). We must put on the mind of Christ in our daily lives for the benefit of having a life with peace. Once I reached a certain level of understanding, God introduced me to the fact that the depth of intercession comes when you begin to understand your foe. When I noticed my brothers and sisters in Christ being delivered from mental breakdowns, from panic attacks, and from anxiety, I was moved to figure out where the entryway was that put them in that state of need.

I would ask questions about deliverance for the sake of spiritual growth. I wanted to sop up every bit of information, as I knew that I would need it as I progressed in my walk with Christ. I was taught that being keen on where demons lodge their presence is important for deliverance.

Again, "Let this mind be in you which was also in Christ Jesus." The "this mind" that is being referenced here is the mind of a servant. The humble mind. The mind of humility and love. It's the belief that *I* am no more deserving than *you*. It is this mind that calls for daily renewing. Why? Because it takes a daily dying of the fleshly mind to keep ahold of the mind that desires to serve rather than be served.

A straightforward approach to understanding the flesh and the Spirit is found in Romans 8:5-6: "For they that are after the flesh do mind the things of the flesh; but they that are after the Spirit the things of the Spirit. For to be carnally minded is death, but to be spiritually minded is life and peace."

These Scriptures give us access to knowledge and understanding so that we can go further into the depths of intercession and make known the spirits that interrupt the lives of many who are working for the Lord.

While there are many evil spirits, I will point out in the next chapter the three more common culprits that come against the believers in Christ Jesus.

In my years of learning to pray, listening to God, and becoming a person of prayer, I have found that most of the intercession that takes place or the prayer requests that are asked of me are on behalf of other believers who have been attacked by these culprits.

"Your armor is a mighty protective suit."

PRAYER

Father, it is in the name of Jesus Christ that I come to you. Thank you for your blessings. I thank you for your provisions. I thank you for meeting my needs and speaking to my spirit. Thank you for your Son who died for my sins. Thank you for the Comforter, the Holy Spirit. Lord, I repent. Please forgive me for my wrongdoings against your will that I have committed knowingly and unknowingly. As I seek to go deeper in your courts, into understanding the battles that lie ahead, I ask that you cover me and protect me. I ask that my faith increases and that my confidence is strong in the power of Jesus. I ask that you guide me through each phase and turn, as I learn more regarding the warfare that is happening in the lives of saints around the world. I pray that I am never without your armor. I pray for the body of Christ that we pray with fervor, wisdom, skill, and, most importantly, the anointing. I pray for your favor as I enter the next level that you are calling me to. I ask all of this in the name of Jesus Christ. Amen.

CHAPTER FIVE

Common Culprits Against the Saints

If we say that we have no sin, we deceive ourselves, and the truth is not in us. If we confess our sins, he is faithful and just to forgive us our sins, and to cleanse us from all unrighteousness.

PRIDE

I mentioned earlier in the book how I had to deal with pride. According to the nature of pride, if I had not been honest with myself, I would be a completely different person today. I still deal with pride, having to rebuke it often, but I am keener to recognizing when it is present as well.

Pride is dangerous and deceitful. One of the ways to deal with pride is to confess your faults. James 5:16 tells us that the point of confession is that it brings about healing. Too often, seasoned saints are headed to the altar because they need healing from something physical or emotional. Often what I've seen and heard is that while at the altar, they are being very vague or general with their prayer request. When asked what it is that they need or want prayer for, the response is almost always, "Just for God to bless me." Or "I just want general prayer."

Maybe you've been that person or have witnessed similar requests. I assure you, I have been that person. And in having been that person, I can minister this to you as wisdom. To be healed, you've got to admit that you need healing.

Being vulnerable is tough for anybody, but Christians tend to struggle with this even after coming to Christ. Why? Because most Christians have already gone through their worldly situations and circumstances and know how people who were considered close to them can mistreat and misuse, and abuse. Many who come to Christ are coming straight from abuse or mistreatment in some form, but are willing to try out this Jesus life.

This is why living a godly life before all men, is so important. We never know who is dealing with what and who is listening and watching us as a godly example.

I struggled with finding other women to confide in because I had heard them gossiping about other saints, and I surely did not want my business out in the neighborhood or in the church. Again, it's difficult to be vulnerable and even more when you are in a noted position of ministry.

A woman confiding in a man who is not her spouse is looked upon as taboo in the church, so that, too, was a no-go. Because of these no-win scenarios, we must understand that pinning the saints into corners of distrust is all a part of the game plan that pride has so cunningly set up against us.

Rather than putting my burdens on someone else, I'd hold on to them and complain to God that these people were fakes and phonies. I didn't even give my issues to Him immediately.

Pride invites shame. In this aspect, pride is the strongman and shame is the worker devil. Pride controls your actions and causes the thoughts of being ashamed to manifest; therefore, the goal of pride is to keep you in a place of denial.

Christians often operate in agreement with pride because pride gives false validation to one's own life. I did this while in conversations after church or just before service where someone would be upset because of the music or the ushering or the whatever, and there I was affirming their pride by saying: "You have every right to feel that way!" or "You know what if it were me..."

The issue with this was that I was comfortable with hearing someone having a bad attitude because I had a bad attitude. I was okay with telling someone they had a right to feel how they felt because I felt frustrated about the way things were going in ministry and in my life.

The Bible declares that pride goes before destruction and a haughty spirit before a fall. After all, it was pride and a haughty spirit that got Lucifer kicked out of heaven (Isaiah 14:12-14).

After being healed of past hurts, I regularly evaluate my attitude to be sure that I am not operating in pride, especially when I am being asked for advice or counsel regarding decisions that affect the lives of others. I do this because I have the testimony that I've come too far to turn back. I'd rather spend time battling against my flesh to prevail against pride than to battle against God!

How Does Pride Manifest?

Pride manifests boldly and sneakily. Pride can be subtle or obvious. Pride can be found in various ways, and it changes with each person. It can show up as a defense mechanism by projecting anger, desperation for attention, or even the neglect of others. Society has given us so many personality traits that pardon pride that we fall prey to this culprit even in our spiritual lives.

If you are introverted or a scholar, you may operate with pride by neglecting to show kindness towards others. This may be done by ignoring them or refusing to bond in the community of Christ. This is masked by statements such as "It's just my personality," or "I'm not a people person," or "They just need to come up to my level; Why should I entertain their ignorance?"

If you're an extrovert, you may operate with pride by displaying the need to be the life of the party. This comes out in comments of "...because no one else will," or "If I'm not doing it, it won't be done, or it won't be done well." We allow pride to dictate who we are when we say, "It's just who I am." God can use anybody and transform any life. But if we are holding on to stank attitudes just because we are unwilling to risk vulnerability, then we are at risk of letting pride rule.

These recent exploits of "who we are" based on personality traits are just another tactic to keep us bound by the spiritual intent of the devils that come after the children of God. When I read the Bible, I do not read it looking for where I fit in per my personality type. The shift in mindset matters because our lives and the lives of others depend on it.

James 4:6 says, "Wherefore he saith, God resisteth the proud, but giveth grace unto the humble." This tells us that God himself comes against the proud.

Examples of pride:

I've been in this church since it started; I'm a founding member with a vote on the board. I deserve and have *earned* the *right* to be in this position. (Entitlement)

It's not my fault no one turned on the heat before service. I'm not the only deacon at this church! (Finding Fault)

How long has she been requesting prayer to stop smoking? You'd think she'd have that under control by now. (Harsh Judgment)

I don't think that this church is right for me; the pastor drives a Toyota, so that must mean the people are broke. (Shallow, Superficial Ideals)

The list could go on, but the point is, pride is not of God. We must be vulnerable and honest enough about our spiritual lack of having the mind of Christ to rid ourselves of this abominable sin.

REJECTION

When rejection happens, it is brought about because of one of two things: self or others.

Whether you are rejecting others or, others are rejecting you. Either way, the feeling of being rejected can be traumatizing.

To experience rejection means that offense took place, and you were left with a feeling of disapproval or unacceptance. Whether it was spoken, written, or acted out, the feeling of "not belonging" or "nobody cares about me" creates a separation in our natural relationships and spiritual relationship with God.

As intercessors, it matters how we deal with a person—whether saved or not—when we pray for them regarding rejection. Remember, a key component to prayer and intercession is humility. It can be enticing to speak in judgment against those who are experiencing rejection by saying phrases such as "Why do you care what others think?" or "If you were mature in Christ, you wouldn't let that keep you from church." A popular statement spoken towards people that are experiencing rejection is, "If people talked about Jesus, what makes you think people won't talk about you?"

While these statements can be factual in context,

the person that is trying to come out from under the bondage of rejection doesn't benefit from hearing them. How you speak to others can make the difference between drawing in and pushing away. Always be willing to check your personal feelings when praying for others or offering counsel. Listen to the Holy Spirit when offering counsel to those that are battling rejection. This spirit causes an emotional response that makes the recipient feel cast aside, unworthy, and it even drives some to feel that they have nothing to live for...no purpose.

If there's anything you've gotten so far from this book, I pray that you get that purpose is the thread of life. It gives every person on the earth their reason for being. Without knowing or understanding purpose, many are walking around in a daze, living without care. Some long so for a purpose, that when they feel there is none, they exit life in an ungodly, untimely manner.

In my battle against rejection, I felt that the stipulations placed on me as a woman regarding attire or leadership in the church were the things that separated me from wanting to formulate relationships with other people in the church. While men are not excluded from dealing with rejection, women tend to battle this culprit in the areas of family matters and church.

In the roles of the home and respect in the household, if women do not feel validated or appreciated, rejection can enter. In the physical church, there may be doctrinal teachings or, sadly, just a matter of opinion amongst fellow Christians that prevent women from feeling at ease with learning and growing or finding their place among the congregants. These uncertainties can cause stagnation in spiritual growth as some find it difficult to see the "point" of attending church.

For men, rejection can occur in similar ways. It often manifests from familial situations for young men who have grown up without a biological parent in the home or who have experienced sexual abuse as a child or teen. Many men struggle to believe that they have a place in the 21st-century church.

In their minds, the church is geared towards women and produces way too much emotion. If these men have become emotionally detached because of a past or present struggle with identity or with being the head of their household or in not receiving validation in their development as a man, going to church can be an issue for them as well.

Christians who have had to deal with the pain of rejection could attest that if the rejection came from a familiar place or a place that is meant to be a safe place, that pain can linger for years. Rejection in the form of church hurt is tough to get out of because the flesh is feeding into the lie that rejection tells.

For some, it may have occurred as a new convert, while for others it happened along the way in their Christian experience. These letdowns make salvation an uphill climb.

Rejection is likened to a mixed martial arts fighter. Inside the ring, the defending fighter makes quick, calculated strikes against their opponent. It is usually when the challenger is against the fence that the defending fighter begins to unrelentingly beat up the opponent. Unleashing rapid kicks and punches, this skilled fighter gains the advantage and ultimately secures the win by not letting up.

Rejection preys on the weak spots in our lives that have yet to be cast upon Jesus or laid at his feet. Rejection uses those weak areas to create insecurities. At this point, we get boxed in, and this is when rejection begins to wail on the emotions and mindset until we give up and are now backsliding.

Matthew 5:10-11 reads, "Blessed are they which are persecuted for righteousness sake: for theirs is the kingdom of heaven. Blessed are ye, when men shall revile you, and persecute you, and shall say all manner of evil against you falsely, for my sake."

To know rejection and the sting of its emotional blow will surely affect your Christian journey. The promises spoken by Jesus Christ prepared us to know how we would be treated by others. In remembering what Scripture says about being persecuted, we can pray and offer wise counsel for the weary and brokenhearted.

DEPRESSION

After having my second child, I underwent a battle with depression. This was not postpartum or baby blues, as it may be called. I can tell you first-hand that you do not have to look sorrowful or pitiful to be depressed. Remember, saints, the battle is to target the mind. I was functional and able to operate. I was prayerful. However, when I was not functioning, operating, or praying, I entered the mind battle.

Being able to remember God's word is a key factor to ward off depression. There is a saying: "Misery loves company." I say, "If misery loves company, depression is the one sending the invites."

A few years before the birth of my second child, I was given a word of encouragement and prophecy by an evangelist. She spoke Psalm 34:19, "Many are the afflictions of the righteous, but God delivereth him out of them all." Oh, how true this is! After hearing this, I grasped it tightly and realized that it would become a Scripture that would forever keep me walking in hope and faith.

In our season of hardship, our afflictions were many. Finances were in and out with the blink of an eye. We had a 2008 Kia Optima with a manual transmission, and when I tell you that this car was a blessing and a blunder, believe me. It was an answer to prayer because we needed transportation, but it was used and came with many headaches. Nearly every morning before going to work, my husband would get up earlier than normal to get the air in the tire because there was a slow leak in the tire. We couldn't afford a new tire, and we couldn't afford a new car, and with time, we couldn't afford to keep putting air in the tire every day, and on many occasions, twice a day.

Naturally, I became desperate. The tactic of depression is to overwhelm the person it targets and do whatever is necessary to create a false narrative.

Yes, my God is a provider. Yes, my Savior is a miracle worker. And yes, we were still trying to get our lives together. I have no shame or issue letting you know that our period of sacrifice was real, and it didn't stop us from trusting and believing in the God of provision.

Too often, we, the children of God, deny our experiences because those experiences seem to go against the interpretation of who Jesus Christ is. We create this romantic story of a hero who died valiantly for his love. Depending on perspective, this is true. But that isn't the perspective that I take on the Son of God. Our earthly issues of despair have nothing to do with God's holiness or Jesus' righteousness. Being in Christ does not stop us from living among the worldly, nor does having Christ prevent us from having to deal with the troubles of this world.

Every time Satan sought to thicken the plot, there would be a measure of grace given to us. It is in these minute breakthroughs—which came in the form of randomly finding a few dollars under the seat of the car or having a tax refund come earlier than expected—that my husband and I were able to catch air. Air allowed us to regain hope and see God in the middle of the mess. Air caused us to breathe a sigh of relief, releasing the burden of the weighted blows that the trials of life hurled at us.

Here is where I must echo Jesus and instruct you to be wise as serpents. When you discover that a brother or sister in Christ is battling depression, pray that the Lord increases their air! As intercessors, compassion helps us to understand the woes of others and helps us to stay mindful of the trials and tribulations that others are facing.

If I have learned anything during our "Job" experience, it is that I was not pardoned from naivety. I was not excused from the hurts of the world. They matured me. They allowed me to know God on another level.

I would like you to know that every test and trial is not meant to be prayed away. However, you must be aware of when the test or trial is an allowance by God for your growth or the growth of whomever you are praying for, or if it is an all-out attack from a demonic spirit.

I learned to keep these common culprits from attacking my life through repentance, forgiveness, and warfare praying. After praying, if the Holy Spirit reveals that the experience is to grow your faith, pray that the Lord will have his way. If the experience is a demonic intrusion, go into warfare mode. I had to learn the difference between a "God is getting my attention" situation and a "the devil is busy" situation.

If the situation was of the latter reason, I learned that even in that, God was able to elevate me.

Release

When you come out of bondage, you often don't think about what made you bound. You're just thankful to be free. When I came out from the attacks of pride, rejection, and depression, I was thankful to be free and ready to learn how to not be bound by those culprits again. This doesn't mean that I will never feel their presence. It means that I have elevated my spiritual understanding to a point where I can tell when a door is ajar, and those culprits are trying to infiltrate my presence and disturb my atmosphere. Therefore, I close the door! I get honest with my shortcomings before the Lord. I have self-evaluation time with the Holy Spirit to find out where I'm off and where I fall short of God's requirements for my life.

When you pray, allow the Holy Spirit to reveal the workers of darkness that war against the saints. God has provided a way out for his children. It is found in righteousness, faithfulness, and repentance. We can change the course of our lives and the lives of others through prayer and righteous living. When the enemy seeks to keep us bound, we can fight back!

"When you pray, allow the Holy Spirit to reveal the workers of darkness that war against the saints."

PRAYER

Father, it's in the name of Jesus Christ that I come to you. I come clearing the way so that my prayers are heard, and the enemy has no right to stand in my way. I repent for my sins known and unknown. I thank you for forgiving me. Father, I believe that you are a Deliverer and a Way Maker. I pray that you would give me the strength to persevere through the tests and trials that are laid before me. I am undergoing a battle, and I believe that you are a very present help in the time of trouble. I pray in the name of Jesus that you allow me to grow in the areas that I am lacking and that I am made strong in the areas that I am weak in. God, you are holy, and your word declares that I am to be holy as you are holy. So now, Lord, I give you total permission to uproot, tear down, and remove from my life everything unholy, unlike you, and unpleasing in your sight. I invite you, Holy Spirit, to fill me anew, refresh my soul, and usher me into my new place in God. I pray these things with faith, believing that not my will but yours be done. In the name of Jesus, Amen.

PRAYER (SPIRIT OF PRIDE)

Spirit of pride, I bind you in the name of Jesus Christ. I bind up your works and manifestations in my life (or the life of the person(s) you are praying for). I cast you away, back to the pits of hell from where you came. I call your works null and void and of no effect. I call on my warring angels to contend with you and to disassemble your chains from off my life (or the life of the person(s) you are praying for). In the name of Jesus, I release a contrite spirit, a humble spirit. I will no longer submit to your will but to the will of my Father in heaven. (Proverbs 16:19)

PRAYER (SPIRIT OF REJECTION)

In the name of Jesus Christ, I bind you, strongman called spirit of rejection. I disown your works, the manifestations of your presence, and all that is associated with you. I am free from rejecting others, rejection by others, self-rejection, and rejecting God. I am no longer your slave. I am a child of God through the spirit of adoption which has called me to be a joint heir to the throne of God. I call on my warring angels to help me overcome this battle. I declare that I am free! I declare that I will carry no residue of your ill-will. I declare that my faith increase and my knowledge in Christ rise! I declare that no weapon formed against me will prosper. In the name of Jesus, I plead the blood of Jesus Christ over my life. You will no longer enslave my thinking. You will no longer impair my vision. I think on those things that are of Christ. I see things the way the Lord would have me to see them. You will not alter my perspective, nor stop my progression. I am not yours! Power belongs to God! I render you powerless in my life. I believe God. I will not allow your false information to weigh me down. I am victorious. It's in the name of Jesus Christ that I pray. Amen. (Romans 8:15)*

PRAYER

In the name of Jesus Christ, I bind you, spirit of depression, that comes to bring heaviness into my life (or the life of the person(s) you are praying for). I bind up your works, your manifestations, and the root cause of your presence. I render you and your works, manifestations, and roots powerless and of no effect. I cast my cares upon the Lord because he cares for me. No longer am I enslaved with doubt, anxiety, fear, wicked thoughts, low self-esteem, or the temptation to give in to your pressures to hurt myself or others, whether verbally, physically, or spiritually. I call on my warring angels in the name of Jesus Christ to run you back to the pit of hell, from where you came. I plead the blood of Jesus Christ over my life (or the life of the person(s) you are praying for). I put on the garment of praise, and I declare that the oil of joy is loosed upon me and causes me to rejoice, causes me to be lifted in spirit, and causes me to receive the Comforter with all his fullness. In the name of Jesus Christ, I declare that I am free from you. I am secure in Jesus, and I am loved by the Father. In the name of Jesus Christ, I pray. Amen. (Isaiah 61:3)

CHAPTER SIX

Changing the Course

For we wrestle not against flesh and blood, but against principalities, against powers, against rulers of the darkness of this world, against spiritual wickedness in high places.

Rootworkers. Voodoo. Black magic. White magic. The practices could go on, but we give no glory to Satan. These names of acts performed by people who operate under demonic influence bear such a weight on the tongue. As a child growing up, those were phrases that weren't unfamiliar, but I thought that they were mostly speculations about a neighbor or the old lady down the road who was mean to kids. I likely dismissed what I heard or saw because it wasn't directly affecting my life at that time. I felt no harm. I was not in a home where these things were being done.

Not being saved, and not really having much knowledge about that lifestyle, I ultimately ignored its reality. After all, it wasn't me. It wasn't my family, and therefore, it wasn't on my radar.

But that's just it. It is a reality. Witchcraft, idolatry, word curses, blood curses, and the practices of the dark world are as much a reality as the wind. You can't see the wind, but you can experience its effect on the surroundings. You can feel the force of nature during hurricane and tornado season. The presence of wind is unmistakably evident. Like the wind, the effects of iniquities, generational curses, and jealousy are deeply related to why many of the things we experience with our loved ones and family members seem overwhelmingly burdensome.

It saddens me to know that there is a thriving business of spiritualists who are being paid to tell willing souls who are thirsty for real connection, something about their life. Some of you reading this may have even had experience in using Tarot cards. These satanic practices have grown in popularity among college students who operate under the thinking of, "It's just a game or something different to do for fun." Communicating with demons should not be done for sport.

As real as it is, maybe dark magic and other satanic practices seem too far-fetched for what you experienced growing up. Possibly, what you experienced was more of a lesser evil. Or at least lesser in terms of our futile thinking. Quite likely, you knew of family members who were alcoholics, adulterers, or victims of domestic violence (or the perpetrator of the act). Later, you may have found yourself down the same path you viewed the family members on, wondering how or why this happened to you.

The open door remains open because no one is closing it by and through prayer. It remains open because of generational disobedience. If you had a childhood of uncommon or unnatural occurrences that were clearly not godly, and you ended up partaking in those practices as you grew older—even if it was on a smaller or lesser scale than what you saw growing up—the fact remains that this was an open door in your life.

Exodus 20:5 reads, "Thou shalt not bow down

thyself to them, nor serve them: for I the LORD thy God am a jealous God, visiting the iniquity of the fathers upon the children unto the third and fourth generation of them that hate me."

God desires that we serve him and him alone. We should not place idols, worldly possessions, and intimate relationships ahead of God. He has already made it clear that because he is a jealous God, the punishment for serving other gods is the result of his wrath upon the family. Throughout the Old Testament, it is clear to see sin occurring in a cyclical pattern, and every so often, one person would come along and break the cycle by obeying and honoring God. That one person was determined, even if but for a season, to change the course.

I am a firm believer in learned behavior. We do what we do because of these two methods: observation or spoken instruction. Observation is a mighty teacher. Being told to "do as I say and not as I do" in terms of not demonstrating the best behavior is a statement that empowers this belief.

I once heard a story of two brothers who grew up in a household where the father smoked cigarettes. One brother grew up and did not smoke. The other brother grew up and did. When the brother who didn't smoke was asked why, he replied, "I grew up watching my father smoke." When the brother who did smoke was asked why his reply was the same: "I grew up watching my father smoke."

It's in stories like this that the power of observation is in effect. The influencers of wickedness know that if you are around wickedness long enough, you'll eventually, in some regard, become subject to the practice. The goal is to appease the flesh. It starts with inquisition. The desire to know what would "really" happen if I went to a psychic. The curiosity behind what liquor "actually" tastes like. If the devil can entice us to the point that the temptation subdues us, then our battle to salvation becomes harder than if we had never entertained those thoughts.

Luke 11:24-26 reads, "When the unclean spirit is gone out of a man, he walketh through dry places, seeking rest; and finding none, he saith, I will return unto my house whence I came out. And when he cometh, he findeth it swept and garnished. Then goeth he, and taketh to him seven other spirits more wicked than himself, and they enter in and dwell there: and the last state of that man is worse than the first."

Getting saved isn't enough. Work goes into keeping the strong man bound. It takes actual effort to keep your soul detached from the powers of darkness, not just a one-time confession of belief, though that's a great start!

If you have once been bound and are now free, HALLELUJAH! Praise God for victory! You know that the power of prayer is real.

As intercessors, we must operate in prayer for the saints with strategy and passion for their deliverance.

PUT IN THE WORK

Demonic spirits know how to target us because they study us, yet many children of God are lacking knowledge concerning the behavior and acts of demons, and intercessors are not excluded. Some don't study spiritual beings because, to be honest, it scares them. We cannot take the grace, grace, grace mentality towards this subject. That type of approach regarding the powers spoken of in Ephesians 6 is to the detriment of the believer.

Yes, God provides grace, but he also provides power. If you think that you won't have to do anything but believe, I'm writing to you, to let you know that intercession takes belief but much more. Remember that even the demons believed, but demons can't be saved! Your faith has to have work put in to cause us to have holy action.

Throughout the years, I have watched numerous deliverance services where men and women are being released from demonic oppression and torment. When the person administering deliverance is learning how that spirit entered in, it is almost always because of a jealous family member, an ongoing generational curse, or through the person that they are in a relationship with or have been in a relationship with. It's terrible to know that family can be the conduit of heartache and torment, but it is true. We cannot idly hope to escape the battle. We must learn how and where to access our help.

It was many years ago that my husband began writing a song based on Psalm 124:7. He would sing it throughout the house, *"Don't let the fowler snare my soul!"* and it would bless me every time he rehearsed that phrase. We must know that the fowlers of this life are planting snares to kill off the children of God by any means necessary. But verse eight of Psalm 124 says, "Our help is in the name of the LORD, who made heaven and earth."

When we call on the name of the Lord, we receive help. Do not take for granted the help that the armies of the Lord can provide. When fighting the devil or devils for the soul of a loved one or for a child of God, or for yourself, the help of our angels surpasses our thinking and our ability. When we call on the Lord, we shift into a new direction, and therefore, we begin to change the course of the blood flow. No longer is that soul subjected to the acts of their family tree. No longer are we fighting against the enemy on our own. We have help!

In my early years of salvation, I used to share with my husband different accounts from my childhood. I would jokingly say, "You better check my bloodline!" to let him know that I came from a family of "*finishers.*"

Today, through salvation and the active works of the Holy Spirit, I declare that same phrase with new meaning. Now, through the blood of Jesus Christ, I am redeemed, and I come in Jesus's name to *finish* off the devil and his lewd attacks against my family and loved ones!

To overcome addiction, to come out of homosexuality, to be freed from abusive relationships that have plagued lives for years—it all requires help. Unity in the body of Christ helps the prayer warrior lock up with other intercessors. Coming into agreement, we combat the demons that have brought forth their wicked devices, manifesting them in the life of the ones we are praying for. We bind that demon and his works.

Once we have shut down the strong man, we then go into deliverance prayers. We rebuke the fowlers that have set the traps for that soul based on the generational bloodline. These prayers are to cover the soul that has been released from the oppression of the demonic attack and to invite the Holy Spirit to minister to them.

As it is to be understood in Ezekiel 18:14-18, no longer will God require the sins of the ancestors to be laid upon the delivered soul. Once they are walking and living in the way of our Lord and Savior Jesus Christ, they are free. Free indeed.

"When the wicked man turneth away from his wickedness that he hath committed, and doeth that which is lawful and right, he shall save his soul alive. Because he considereth and turneth away from all his transgressions that he hath committed, he shall surely live, he shall not die" (Ezekiel 18:27-28).

As intercessors, we can change the course through prayer, fasting, and teaching. As a person under affliction, you can change the course of your life by turning your heart to God.

When we call on the Lord for help, we can see deliverance and we can win souls back from the enemy. If you are currently praying for a soul that is troubled by generational curses and strongholds, do not give up. Suit up, link up, and call on your help!

"Our soul is escaped as a bird out of the snare of the fowlers: the snare is broken, and we are escaped" (Psalm 124:7).

Prayer

Father, it's in the name of Jesus Christ that I come to you. I thank you, for you are holy. You are righteous. You are merciful. Thank you for your love and your kindness. I come to you asking that you forgive me for my sins—for the things that I did against your will knowingly, and for the things that I did against your will unknowingly. I come to you asking that your will be performed in my life. I no longer give myself over to my will. Your word declares that I do not have to be a partaker of the sins of my father. I choose this day to walk the walk of faith. I put my trust in you, Heavenly Father. I believe in your divine will for my life, and I seek you to understand my purpose. I plead the blood of Jesus over my life, and I pray for your angels of protection to go before me and behind to guard and protect me. I believe in the power of the Holy Spirit, and I pray that your precious anointing will be poured upon my head that I may receive strength and the ability to walk without wavering in my faith. I ask you in the mighty name of your Son, Jesus Christ. Amen.

CHAPTER SEVEN

Moving in the Presence

For he satisfieth the longing soul, and filleth the hungry soul with gladness.

As expressed throughout the book thus far, being an intercessor is a calling that requires much from you naturally and spiritually. As discussed in the previous chapter, contending against strongholds, generational curses, and demonic activity is work. And for that work, we need help. Executing spiritual deliverance can be a lengthy and exhausting situation.

While under the anointing in prayer, you may not feel exhausted. Likewise, you are certainly not mindful of time. However, it is when you are no longer under the power of the anointing that your physical body becomes drained and in need of replenishing.

It is not uncommon to experience a season of rest after vigorous bouts in prayer. This doesn't mean that you are completely disengaged. It simply means that you are not currently on the front lines. Throughout the years, I have had seasons of rest such as this. I found myself entering one of those seasons again while writing this book. This time of reflection and listening was welcomed. It allowed me the room to access the necessary information for the next assignment in my spiritual walk, so I thought.

It was during this time that I began to reflect on my personal living and not just on my spiritual. I reflected on my home, my family, my acquaintances, and even my former acquaintances.

I started looking around the natural side of life and began to feel dissatisfied. I was missing that "get up and go" mentality towards my personal life. One evening, I was in conversation with my husband, and I realized that frustration and discontentment were accompanying me. Being at the point of wanting to be rejuvenated and not feeling rejuvenated brings about weariness.

After sharing my feelings, I settled myself long enough to receive wise counsel from my spouse and hear what the Spirit had to say. This is when I clearly heard the Holy Spirit say again, *"If you can go through it, someone else can relate to it."*

Many intercessors were quite likely going through a similar experience. I was supposed to be in a season of recuperation, and here I was dragging my feet in my domestic responsibilities. I felt unaccomplished. More than that, I didn't know how to recalibrate. I gathered that this was another nudge for a turn of seasons. Well, one thing is sure, when it's time to change, intercessors feel it before they see it. We tend to operate in a different language. Sometimes all that needs to be said is, "I feel something happening." We don't always have the right words to describe what we see or feel, but we know that it's happening spiritually. Often, with spiritual matters, things can change and are known to change based on how we pray.

Therefore, we find ourselves trying to process spiritual foreknowledge or future occurrences, and that information can be difficult to speak on or we are not permitted to share at all. This, as you may already know, is another peculiar trait that many intercessors experience and is common among prophetic intercessors. This peculiarity also made this a trying experience.

The more I tried to get over this, the more of a burden I began to feel. I had specific requests before the Lord, and in making my requests known, I was led to think, "How could I spend time in prayer and not dedicate that same energy to my home?"

Understand this: I don't mind sharing with you the battles, the pain, and the strife of the spiritual affairs of being an intercessor. That is common ground for us. But getting into my house, my living quarters, and my personal space seems rather...personal. In my guarded opinion, this is unnecessary.

However, the Holy Spirit is an excellent teacher. He prodded me until I said yes and started writing. I look at it now and see that, by saying yes, this was another opportunity to build that very real, very honest connection with intercessors and saints alike. So, I released my fingers to continue the task.

POWER OF TRANSPARENCY

Here it is. The unfiltered truth. I struggle with being an intercessor and maintaining discipline in other areas of my life. To some, that may not be a big deal. To me, it is. Why? Because I believe that God grants the desires of my heart, and this is a desire of mine. I teach my children to be good stewards over what God has given them, and it is a basic principle to practice what you preach. Remember in the first few chapters how I shared with you that I had completely different plans for my life? Well, the thought of trying to accomplish and maneuver my desires still lingers, and every now and again, they pop up to test my will. As I've said, I must yield completely to His will for my life, and if I don't, I experience times of stagnation and frustration. Therefore, learning to die to the flesh daily is a part of the Christian journey.

I know what it means to pray and fast and suffer in my body for the sake of someone or something outside of myself. Yet, maintaining the balance that abundant living provides has proven to be a headache all its own, and it sneaks up on you, causing discomfort in the body. I dare not say, "Don't judge me," because there's no reason to say that. If you are reading this book, then you are likely a sincere Christian who wouldn't dare think to pass judgment on another. *Right?*

Clearly, I'm aware that many of you reading this have already concluded where this subject stands with you.

But seriously, this is my real life, not the expert's guide to prayer or the wonderful walk of being in love with Jesus.

This means that there are days the dishes are not cleaned, laundry is washed but not put away, and dinner is whatever works. This doesn't mean my home is falling apart or that my kids are feasting on candy bars for dinner. It means that I had to find a way to be okay with not having a staged kitchen or a photoshoot-ready living room. I had to be okay with raising children who may not always understand the responsibilities that are placed on them because of who their parents are. It means that the sacrificial part of the intercessory ministry isn't all wrapped up in the spirit realm, even though there are spiritual implications and revelations attached to the natural side of this call.

Why share this? What's the point? It doesn't seem all that spiritually necessary, right? The point of me sharing this is because the same reason that I didn't want to share it coincided with how I felt about my spiritual discipline. Most intercessors tend to keep a low profile on their private lives. The nature of our spiritual work seems to demand there be a separation. It goes without saying that the workload behind all that wonderful praying can be underestimated.

This can be even more strenuous when you're the spouse of someone who pastors or heads an organization, or when your family is taking on more responsibility within your own familial dynamic such as caring for an elderly parent or loved one with a handicap, or when the family agenda has shifted throughout the community and you are starting a new business, or when your responsibilities at work have increased. The personal curves of life can and often do coincide with your spiritual growth. The great sacrifice of praying with anointing and fervor regarding your purpose and trying to balance work and home makes it easy to understand how the latter can get lost in the fray.

Here I was in a period of rest yet finding myself feeling restless. Why didn't I have the energy to put into my home or my personal well-being? The question of *why* became the motivation to seek out what was really going on spiritually. I was in my spiritual time of recuperation, but naturally, I was juggling different tasks throughout the day, such as writing, school schedules, travel schedules, and ministry. I was running and doing but feeling mundane and bland.

Lively Stones, Even at Home

Constantly drained and keeping up with upkeep was unsatisfactory. I was tired. This is what I call "too much to do and not enough time to do it." In describing how I felt, I liken it to what I call saltine cracker syndrome. The saltine cracker is associated with being sick. It is offered to buffer the need for solids on the stomach while you are unable to keep down more substantial foods. It isn't the main course. It's nothing memorable or satisfying. The palate doesn't desire or crave a saltine cracker. It serves only to get the stomach and digestive system to the desired functioning ability. The goal is to be well enough to eat a more substantial meal. I desired to experience the greater, more substantial meal. I wasn't completely tasteless; there was salt, that was clear. However, there was only just enough salt to say that there was salt. There was no progression.

A few years back during our time with a deliverance ministry, my husband and I were told that we must have a pure heart to operate and function in ministry. My home is also my ministry. I wanted to get into the presence of God and experience His restorative power. To do that, I had to have a pure heart.

Matthew 5:8 reads, "Blessed are the pure in heart: for they shall see God." It takes consecration and sanctification to get and keep a pure heart. Both require elimination. To align with God's desires for our life based on what the Holy Spirit tells us can be challenging because our flesh is never in agreement with the Spirit.

The promise in verse eight is that the pure in heart shall see God. Understanding the Scripture on a spiritual plane is not difficult. However, naturally, one could argue that no man has seen God and lived. Yet, as intercessors, we know that we have both seen God and are yet able to tell about it. How? In the miracles that have been performed in the lives of those who we pray for. In the deliverance from demonic spirits and in the fulfillment of the promise of the Holy Ghost. And more astonishingly, in the miracle of our day-to-day life—breathing, seeing, walking, talking. Seeing God isn't meant only when we enter heaven's gates. I desire to see God in every area of my life. Especially within my home.

As I began evaluating my spiritual health, I realized that I wasn't seeing him in every area, and I became dissatisfied with the results. I was losing the vigor, zeal, and attention span to sit and wait for the Lord. I was out of focus. But God is merciful! When I got honest with myself, I began to take issue with how I became stale, outdated, and near the point of drying out, I was able to recognize that I was on autopilot. I was able to acknowledge my shortcomings. I had enough sense to know that this was not where I should be.

The frustration I experienced naturally was in clear relation to my spiritual frustration. After many days of conversation with God, the Holy Spirit spoke to me, letting me know that I was going through elevation. I was taken by surprise. Usually, I can sense when I'm shifting to a different level. This time, I only sensed that something was going on. In the middle of acknowledging my struggle and my need for a change, I got elevated. It seems strange, right? But it is certainly not!

I'd like to say this in case someone doesn't know it or hasn't realized it yet: if you are praying for God to elevate you and use you and, I dare to say, "make you great," I'd like to demystify the notion that when you receive your elevation, it's going to be something grand. Not on this side of heaven, at least. Elevation is work. The reward of obedience is more work. The idea of greatness means more work. Our mentalities about being used by God should not be set on earthly gain or glory.

The blessings that are poured out upon us as we

are elevated, matured, and advanced can yield natural fruit, but what is required is more work towards the kingdom of heaven to maintain and be good stewards over those blessings.

More responsibility, more time, and more sacrificing are what elevation ultimately means. If you're evangelizing, that may result in more territory to cover. If you're pastoring, that may mean more sheep entering the fold, which in turn means more praying, protecting, and teaching. If you're a prophet, that may mean more time before his throne and in his word.

As an intercessor, I share this with you because I had to learn this through the hard knocks of life in and out of the physical church. Please keep this in mind as we are praying for others. We do not want to pray something for someone without praying God's provision for them to be successful in that thing.

As I started the evaluation process for this elevation, I was led to the conclusion that more stillness, more quietness in conversation, more praying and seeking, and more fasting was my portion.

Elevation required me to enter a new consecration. Please understand that as God grows you, you can expect your responsibilities to grow. And it goes without saying—but it never hurts to hear it from a fellow intercessor—that not everyone will take kindly to the turning away or turning down of invitations because they are often left out of knowing the reason behind why you can't stay or why you can't go. I usually do not share with anyone but my spouse the details surrounding my consecration. If someone is privileged to know, then it is truly a privilege.

Again, as persons of prayer, we tend to be relatively private people regarding our personal lives, but not only is that a reason for not sharing everything regarding your consecrations, but I also learned not to cast my pearls before swine (Matthew 7:6). Not everyone is entitled to your spiritual jewels, and not everyone cares to engage in what it takes for you to get to where you are going.

Because I had been doing and transitioning in different capacities that kept my mind on the needs of others and not considering what my soul needed, I ended up missing the cues and clues that I was about to enter a new area of my walk. However, through this, I gained knowledge of something I didn't know. I learned that the Holy Spirit shifts even if we don't. Therein lies the frustration. I felt that something either needed to change or had changed, but I was obliviously going through the motions.

Here's where many of you may have an "ah-ha" moment. The Holy Spirit would not allow me to keep this to myself, because this speaks to so many people all over the globe—no gender exclusivity here. Again, your gender doesn't stop you from being an intercessor. Here's the truth: we cater, wait on, serve, and almost live for our spouses, children, church affiliations, memberships, congregants, groups, family, and friends. So much so that we seemingly neglect our own needs. This isn't new information; it's just me pointing out that even the most noted information can be overlooked in your own life. It was overlooked in my life.

So, I did what intercessors do. I detected the problem, found the source of it, and prayed for the solution. The results were clear. I needed a soul-stirring, personal revival.

I began to seek the Lord for his presence so that I could *see* him. I didn't want to enter the next level dry and stale and on the verge of burnout. I wanted living waters to flow freely again. I wanted God to welcome me into His presence. After all, He didn't need to be renewed; I did. This wasn't about inviting him into *my* presence. I wanted God to invite me into his.

When I pushed myself to move beyond my staleness, I withheld nothing from the Lord. I asked what I needed to do to come from this dry place. I used practical knowledge to revitalize my health and my energy and to plan appropriately for my domestic responsibilities, all so that I could continue to thrive in both the natural and spiritual places.

I came to the point where the learned lesson was that while I strove for the well-kept home, the best-behaved children, and the awe-inspiring love story of a marriage, I had to equally strive for a well-kept soul, the best discipline in my character, and an awe-inspiring, never-dying testimony of God's love for me.

As time ticked away, I became more disciplined, praise God! I enjoyed my time of rest much more. I re-focused my time and energy on things that were purposeful and that were going to impact the lives of others. This was work, but the point of revival is so that we can continue to work. It is a refreshing that occurs so that we, the children of God, can go out and do the work that is set before us for the space of time allotted to do it in. And so, it was. In this season of rest, the Holy Spirit ushered me into the presence of God. My request had been granted.

Moving in the presence of God takes you out of character. Your normal self, as known by yourself or by others. We cannot move into the holiest presence there is and remain the same. As He moves, your body takes on a new tolerance, and you feel the indescribable. Your mouth takes on a new tongue, and you speak a different degree of the unknown. Your vision enhances. You develop and mature spiritually. Naturally, you may look the same, you may even sound the same, but spiritually, you have elevated once again.

First Chronicles 16:8-10 instructs us, "Give thanks unto the LORD, call upon his name, make known his deeds among the people. Sing unto him, sing psalms unto him, talk ye of all his wondrous works. Glory ye in his holy name: let the heart of them rejoice that seek the LORD."

For you who are intercessors, you know the overflowing joy that comes when our requests are granted by the Father. We leap, we run, we shout, we wave our hands, we cry, and we do whatever our bodies can produce as a gesture of our gratitude. I did all of it. I was thankful and shall forever be thankful for the great and mighty God that I serve.

First Chronicles 16:27 reads, "Glory and honour are in his presence; strength and gladness are in his place."

I delight in knowing that there is honor in the presence of God. To be beckoned to come, even when I think I've fallen short or have missed the practical mark, shows that he still provides me the honor of his presence. When my body seemed to need much rest and restoration in his place, where He is, I was able to draw and experience His strength.

To convey all that the Holy Spirit would have you to know has been a challenge for me. The word of God alone at times isn't enough. Experience to apply what we believe can help another soul get through their own experience that they have no words for. I believe that the transparency of my struggles on the natural side of life as a wife and mother offers encouragement to those of you who are parents, married or not.

Though I am not advocating for the dismissal of your home life, I am shining light that if you see yourself overwhelmed or dissatisfied in your natural abode or area of work, there is more than likely a spiritual check-up that must happen.

In the 21st century, taking care of domestic affairs can seem antiquated. However, there are great spiritual significances to having a place where you can freely enter and abide in the spirit realm without the stumbling blocks of natural distractions.

Don't allow the enemy to use your dwelling, your job, or any of your natural situations as a spiritual hindrance. If he can get us distracted from the move of God long enough, we will find ourselves perturbed with our circumstances and loved ones and being distant without cause. Don't be a sucker for Satan. Don't let him use you. He doesn't care how he gets you off course. He is a deceiver and is known to come against us in every kind of way.

There's a saying, "If you let him ride, he'll want to drive." Therefore, don't even stop to pick him up! Keep moving forward in everything the Lord has caused your hands to have access to and you'll find that He will allow you to move into His presence without limitation or hesitation.

"As God grows you, expect your responsibilities to grow."

PRAYER

Heavenly Father, in the name of Jesus Christ I come before you to offer thanksgiving. Thank you for showing me my shortcomings. Thank you for allowing me the opportunity to do better and be better in the life that you have blessed me with. I do not take for granted the blessings of my life. I appreciate all that you have given me, and even when I do not properly care for those aspects of my life, you are merciful and gracious. Thank you for the power of the Holy Spirit who is my Comforter when I am overwhelmed and my Teacher when I need instruction. When I am missing the mark in my personal affairs, he leads me to you. He brings clarity to my understanding and my thinking. He provides for me a new perspective and spiritual insight that I need to live the life that you've blessed me to have. I pray in the name of Jesus Christ that you will continue to overflow in my life. In every area of my life, I declare that your blessings are flowing, and I declare that I will not be my own stumbling block. Thank you for your patience with me. Your mercy endures forever. You are the Sovereign God and there is none like you in all the earth. I give you praise. It's in Jesus's name that I pray. Amen.

FOREVER

If you are always trying to be normal you will never know how amazing, you can be.

−Maya Angelou

CHAPTER EIGHT

Dependency

> *You will keep in perfect and constant peace the one whose mind is steadfast [that is, committed and focused on You—in both inclination and character] because he trusts and takes refuge in You [with hope and confident expectation].*

As intercessors and children of God, we are already leaning on the teachings of Jesus Christ. But there comes a point of no-holds-barred faith, where we will need Jesus beyond the red text. Many of us already know this and have experienced times of needing him in a pressing kind of way.

Needing something or someone outside of your own ability to function is called dependency. On a considerably basic level, we all depend on something or someone else for our daily living.

For me, experiencing unexpected elevation came with the immediate need to lean on Jesus even more. During this time, I was careful to let Jesus know just how needy I had become. I spoke with him regarding the present, the future, matters of great faith, and things that were daily tasks. I was revived, and I knew that my workload was about to increase. To get to where the Lord was commanding me to go, I had to not only depend on him but on his people as well.

Depending on other brothers and sisters in Christ exposed me to the way God must view us when it comes to loving thy neighbor.

There are so many Christians who are still dealing with some of the culprits that were mentioned in Chapter Five, and it is difficult for them to lend themselves to anyone but themselves. Their perception of other Christians is so full of cataracts that they are not seeing beyond the hurts that they have personally experienced.

As a person who knows what it is like to jumble every person who has misused you into the no-good, no-use pile, I can tell you that you cannot reciprocate hate and walk with God. There's no way. We need each other, and we need to know that our need for each other is biblical.

In Matthew 22:39 we are told to love our neighbor as ourselves. This wasn't a suggestion. It was a microscopic look at the fact that if we are willing to feed ourselves, clothe ourselves, comfort ourselves with entertainment, then we are required to pass along that same love to others.

Jesus needed the disciples to teach these principles so that they in turn could teach others. I have heard some argue that not everybody is your neighbor and not every person is your brother or sister in Christ. This is true, as the Bible clearly indicates that some are of their father, the devil. Yet, I extend this invitation to you, that we utilize discernment, common sense, and compassion to strengthen the kingdom and keep the body of Christ well.

BE WISE

Consider this: our great intercessor, who is the epitome of the sacrificial ministry of intercession, called Judas Iscariot to be one of his disciples, one of the original twelve. He walked and talked and ate with the same man who chose silver rather than the Savior. Jesus's stance on the matter remained. He knew that this would bring about the fulfillment of his purpose.

Likewise, inviting others to share a part of your work or ministry will always present the possibility of there being a Judas in the camp. But, as our Savior demonstrated, we can know the intentions of a person and not be moved. It didn't take long for Judas to realize that he made a grave mistake.

Scripture tells us that God will make our enemies our footstools. Having a Judas allowed Jesus to progress to the point of his purpose. Remember, we are to be wise as serpents and harmless as doves. Don't let the enemy put restraints on your relationships. Even Satan knows that there is strength in numbers, which is why he is trying to keep the children of God fighting each other instead of the principalities and wickedness that he is conjuring up. Remember that alienation is deception.

We aren't in competition with one another. Despite what all the social norms may subconsciously be feeding us. We are not each other's enemy. Common among everyone nowadays is the hustle mentality, the grind mentality, and the do-it-better-than-anyone-else mentality. These are mentalities that force us to think that we don't need others, but the reality is that we do. To make it in any aspect of your Christian journey, you will need others and you do not need to be in competition for God's attention.

While leaning in this season of dependency, I was reminded of 2 Samuel 23:8-16. In this passage of Scripture, we find that David and his army are trapped in a cave surrounded by the Philistines. Among the men are three skilled warriors by the names of Adino, Eleazar, and Shammah. Each man has his own record that proves his skill and why he is known as chief amongst the rest.

What astounds me here is that when David desired a drink from the well of Bethlehem, which was by the gate, those three men broke through the Philistines and drew out water from the well and brought it back to David. Those men took upon themselves the need of David and put their skill to work, going out against the Philistines, risking their lives to get water, and fighting their way back to keep the water intact until it reached its place of destination.

The amazing thing about this is that it didn't matter who had more battle wins, who had been fighting the longest, or who had more experience with the sword. They worked with each other, untouched by the potential threat of egos taking over.

As brothers and sisters in Christ, I pray that we are embracing the King's plea and joining arms with one another to accomplish the set goal of spreading the Gospel, without regard to our personal accomplishments, accolades, and egos.

We have a set time on this planet, and no man knows the day or the hour in which we will be taken away. We have so much work set before us, and yet we do not have a guarantee of the time in which we have to accomplish that work. We have heard about the end times, we have read about it, and we've even seen movies about it. Let us not haphazardly operate in the things of God and misuse the opportunities that are presented to us.

Don't be foolish, but don't let fear be the excuse used to stay inactive and disengaged.

Our dependence on Christ Jesus must be so unconditional that we do not fear to go beyond comfort zones and be the peculiar creatures we were created to be. We must act wisely and walk circumspectly, not being ignorant of the issues that arise in our lives, but also not letting those issues become our lives. We depend on knowledge and faith to bring forth great peace and victory in a time of spiritual disruption. I learned and will always be learning that I am my best when I am at my lowest in self-righteousness and am in a constant mode of dependency on Christ Jesus.

> *"Don't be foolish, but don't let fear be the excuse used to stay inactive and disengaged."*

PRAYER

Father, in the name of Jesus Christ, I thank you for being a sure foundation. I thank you for being the solid rock. Thank you for teaching me that I cannot make it in this world on my own. I pray that the intercessors who are joining me in prayer are blessed to keep praying and fighting and teaching and speaking and sowing and declaring and doing what the Holy Spirit is calling for us to do in this time of our lives. I pray for the people of God who are called to prayer but are stuck in the battle of deliverance from hurt and rejection and doubt. God, I pray that if not these words, that someone will speak the right words that can pierce through the stony heart. I pray in Jesus's name that we as people of prayer continue to find ourselves leaning on you as every round goes higher and higher. God, I pray that no amount of success, fame, or status will ever be able to remove your servants from having a humble spirit. Let us not forget that it is because of you that we can achieve and do and have whatever successes we may attain. It's in the name of Jesus Christ that I pray. Amen.

CHAPTER NINE

Confidence for the Journey

Do not, therefore, fling away your [fearless] confidence, for it has a glorious and great reward.

While I traveled from circumstance to situation on my journey of becoming an intercessor, I learned to pack differently for each location of transition. One of the most important things I kept in my spiritual suitcase was my confidence in God.

Once you have an experience with Jesus, it's never easy to let go of the changes that take place in your life. I have been striving to tell of His goodness and to demonstrate His love everywhere I go and on every platform, I am blessed to be on.

The journey that is yet set before us requires patience and much prayer. The times of tests and trials are heavily upon us as a people. Many things have occurred while writing this book and I am sure that many things will occur when this book is published. In all of the different social, political, racial, and even religious matters, we shall not be moved.

If we want to receive and enjoy what God promises us, we must do His will. We have to be confident in what He instructs and careful to carry out His plan accordingly. Being authentically who God has called you to be, helps you thrive in the things that God has called you to do.

I used to think that my voice sounded weird, or that I didn't have the look of a minister's wife or of an evangelist. I thought that I had to wear a suit everywhere or sound deep in every conversation. Granted, while I have been known to be called *deep*, I am not set out to be something I'm not.

Being who you are and walking confidently in the authority that God has granted you is for you to know how to live this life in Christ in abundance and thrive. To understand your God-given purpose and be in pursuit of that is fulfilling.

Intercessors, watchmen, prayer warriors, and

those who are generals of the faith, walk confidently with God and dwell in the place of provision that he has allotted you.

CHAPTER TEN

Forever Changed

> *But the God of all grace, who hath called us unto his eternal glory by Christ Jesus, after that ye have suffered a while, make you perfect, stablish, strengthen, settle you.*

Many years have since passed from my first noted spiritual experience at my baptism. Since then, I have grown in ways that are immeasurable and I have encountered more spiritual occurrences than I could have ever imagined. I have fellowshipped in a variety of places of worship. I have met many different people along the way, and I have had many circumstances and situations that have shaped me in ways that I would have never thought possible.

Throughout the fellowships, the diverse churches, the plethora of life's blows, and the ongoing changes that occur, I am forever changed by the unchanging nature of Jesus Christ. As a child, I didn't know him; I couldn't understand the thought of him being more than a picture on a wall or a character in the Bible.

As a teenager, I began to learn of him, get acquainted with him, and really develop a desire for him. I stumbled and I lost energy during the race, but I eventually crossed over the line. As a young adult, I loved him; I found him intriguing and fascinating and spectacular, and to be the helper of my shortcomings and the ruler of my rights. During all my unforeseen circumstances of yesterday, Jesus was constant.

As an adult, I know him more intimately, more personally, more than by name, more than by red letter, more than by song or thought. I am completely dependent upon his living and resurrection to make my life what it is purposed to be. I am completely in awe of the majesty that is known as His glory. Today, Jesus is my King. He is the never-failing intercessor that has given me determination, passion, and persistence. He keeps me being the me that the Father created me to be.

When I wanted to write books, I believed that I was going to publish a line of children's books. I had been working on ideas and concepts, and I believed that it was going to be what God wanted for me. One day, unexpectedly, I was told differently by the Holy Spirit. Not that I was not to produce children's books, but that I must do this book first. I had no idea where this book was coming from at that time. I had a different timeline to release this work. But as I obeyed the Holy Spirit, here it is.

I remember feeling frustrated at one point in my marriage. I was a young wife who was married to a man in ministry, and I would tell my husband that I had no one to relate to. I didn't know any other young women during this time who could understand what I was going through as a twenty-something-year-old, as a mom, as a wife. There were no books or books that I could find, and no one was talking about the struggles of being married to someone in ministry while in ministry or while parenting. It was a silent market.

I remember always being the youngest woman in the fellowships of ministers' wives. Some women were older than me, but as I listened for wisdom, I always came up empty-handed. When you are married to a person who is called by God to see and to hear and to declare the mysteries of God, you mature in spiritual things quickly and differently. This book is the answer to the questions that I would often ask my husband, such as "Who could relate to what I'm going through?"

If you have ever asked this question—or a question similar in nature—I pray that, through the pages of this book, you have concluded that you are not alone. There is someone out there who gets it. You have an overflowing teacup of anointed men and women who are on your side and who are praying for you because you are called to intercession. They are praying for you because you are a child of the Sovereign God. They are praying for you because it is their call to do so.

I pray that men and women around the world will continue to lift the banner and pray unashamedly and unafraid because of the things that I have given voice to in this book. I pray that your daily domestic life is no longer looked upon as a headache, but that you relate with honesty to those who are experiencing the realness of day-to-day living and encourage them to give even the dishes over to God. Let the Holy Spirit teach you how to schedule and plan. Strategizing for kingdom living isn't only for spiritual things.

There are so many reasons to give God praise, and so many, many people that have touched my life. I know that I am the product of prayer. In all the unknown roads that lie ahead, and with great expectation, I know that in all of it, Jesus will remain constant.

As I shared with you at the beginning of this work, the aim isn't to give you my life's story, but rather, my life's purpose, so that your story may be one of fulfillment in your call. However different or similar, as an intercessor, I believe that our lives are in some way connected.

My desire is that my transparency has allowed you to grow even more in Christ and as a mighty warrior in prayer.

If I could say anything else to aid in your walk, it would be this: My goal is to bridge the gap between life and prayer. There are so many people of God who are failing at life because of the blows that it gives. Life and prayer do not sit separately; they are jointly fitted. Do not let life be the reason you stop praying. For it is because of life that we must always find ourselves praying to hear, to see, to do, and to deliver.

I have learned and will forever be learning. I have grown and will forever be growing. I have changed and will forever be changed. I am blessed because Jesus Christ has remained constant. He is the same yesterday, today, and forever.

Jesus Christ the same yesterday, and today, and forever. Hebrews 13:8

***

Remember

by Brittany Smalls

There are days that I don't want to

then I think of all there is to do

Remember the lost, remember the weak, remember those who have great needs

There are times when I don't want to

then I think of all there is to do

Remember the mothers, remember the fathers, remember those who have neither

There are moments when I just don't want to

then I remember those who need me to:

The sick, the lame, the blind, the defeated

The hungry, the hurting, the poor in spirit

The left out, the forgotten, the impoverished, the spoiled-rotten

The no-goods, the too-goods, the wish-they-could-do-goods

The hopeless, the depressed, the oppressed, the stressed

The afflicted, the ashamed, the rejected

Those addicted to pain

The kidnapped, the trafficked

The ones fighting opioid habits…

There are days that I don't want to. Then, I remember

I remember all of you

I remember what He's called me to.

About the Author

Brittany V. Smalls is a Christian author, blogger, and orator of prayer. She releases honesty and inspiration through her writing. Working towards bridging the gap between life and prayer, Smalls writes to encourage others through the difficulties of life while following Christ. In her book, *Yesterday, Today, and Forever – The Sacrificial Ministry of Intercession*, she highlights the journey of her first Christian experience to her Godly purpose. Smalls grew up in South Carolina as the youngest of three daughters and is thankful to be a wife and mother.

For book purchases, speaking engagements, and more information, please visit:
www.brittanysmalls.com

www.ingramcontent.com/pod-product-compliance
Lightning Source LLC
Chambersburg PA
CBHW060533100426
42743CB00009B/1521